OXFORD

CHORAL
CLASSICS

Madrigals and Partsongs

EDITED BY CLIFFORD BARTLETT

SERIES EDITOR
JOHN RUTTER

T0347615

MUSIC DEPARTMENT

OXFORD
UNIVERSITY PRESS

OXFORD
UNIVERSITY PRESS

Great Clarendon Street, Oxford OX2 6DP, England
198 Madison Avenue, New York, NY10016, USA

Oxford University Press is a department of the University of Oxford.
It furthers the University's aim of excellence in research, scholarship,
and education by publishing worldwide in

Oxford New York
Auckland Cape Town Hong Kong Karachi
Kuala Lumpur Madrid Melbourne Mexico City Nairobi
New Delhi Shanghai Taipei Toronto

With offices in

Argentina Austria Brazil Chile Czech Republic France Greece
Guatemala Hungary Italy Japan Poland Portugal Singapore
South Korea Switzerland Thailand Turkey Ukraine Vietnam

ISBN 0-19-343694-9 978-0-19-343694-7

Music originated on Sibelius
Printed in Great Britain on acid-free paper by
Halstan & Co. Ltd., Amersham, Bucks.

CONTENTS

PREFACE

The aim of the *Oxford Choral Classics* series is to offer choirs a practical and inexpensive working library of standard repertoire in new, reliable editions. Where space allows, music that is less widely known but of special value within its genre is also included. Inevitably, any anthology is a personal selection reflecting the perspective of its editor, and it must also be recognized that there are wide national differences in repertoire: what is standard fare for a choir in one country may be little known in another. For this volume of madrigals and partsongs it has been a hard task to narrow down the enormous field of marvellous music to fit a 384-page book. In general, I have selected those pieces which are regarded as classics of their kind and which I have sung with pleasure over the years in a variety of different amateur vocal ensembles. I have deliberately included three lengthy items—Debussy's *Trois Chansons*, Monteverdi's *Lamento d'Arianna*, and Vaughan Williams's *Three Shakespeare Songs*—to counterbalance the brevity of many of the other pieces. I hope that those whose singing has been confined to the English language will enjoy the French, German, and Italian items. For historical reasons, the book has, chronologically, rather a hollow centre. During the seventeenth and eighteenth centuries, most vocal music required the accompaniment of at least a harpsichord, as is shown by the Monteverdi pieces here: nos. 38 and 39 had continuo parts added in later editions, while no. 40 had one from the start. Writing for unaccompanied mixed voices resumed only in the nineteenth century. One area that is under-represented is nineteenth-century Germany. Those wishing to explore that repertoire more fully can do so from *German Romantic Partsongs*, selected and edited by Judith Blezzard (Oxford University Press, 1993). Other Oxford anthologies covering specific areas in more depth are: Philip Ledger, *Oxford Book of English Madrigals* (1978); Alec Harman, *Oxford Book of Italian Madrigals* (1983); Frank Dobbins, *Oxford Book of French Chansons* (1987); and Paul Hillier, *English Romantic Partsongs* (1986).

The specific parameters followed for selection here have been these:

1. The period covered is from about 1500 up to the twentieth century (though copyright considerations have limited the amount of twentieth-century music included).
2. Music for male or for female voices has been excluded, as have settings of folksongs (though nos. 1, 28, and 50 may fall into that category) and American music. These may be included in future volumes of the series.
3. The music included comes from England, France, Germany, and Italy (with one partially Spanish piece to open the book).
4. Only complete, self-standing compositions have been included. There are two items which may seem to be exceptions: Elgar's *As torrents in summer* (no. 14), a self-sufficient partsong from *King Olaf* and subsequently circulated independently, and Monteverdi's *Lamento d'Arianna* (no. 40), which the composer arranged from the solo operatic version.

This volume contains music from several traditions. The French polyphonic chanson and the Italian madrigal both arose in the 1520s. The fact that the repertoire circulated so widely in print implies that there must have been a market of enthusiastic singers throughout western Europe (and beyond: records survive of the regular dispatch of the latest editions from Venice to a customer in Poland). In England, the craze for madrigal singing was inspired by the importation of Italian books in the 1580s and encouraged by Thomas Morley's publications in the 1590s. Germany had its own native tradition, which gradually absorbed Italian traits. In the early years of the seventeenth century, this sort of singing declined. Solo music became more fashionable. In England it was supplemented by music for male voices sung in convivial surroundings.

Most sixteenth-century vocal music was essentially for ensembles of soloists. But when it was revived (a process that in England went back to the madrigal societies of the mid-eighteenth century), it was sung chorally, and new repertoire was written for larger ensembles. A century ago, Elgar's partsongs may well have been regularly sung by choirs of two hundred. Over the last few decades, such choirs have tended to concentrate on large-scale choral works, leaving madrigals and partsongs to smaller choirs. All the music in this collection works when sung chorally; the madrigals may, of course, be sung with single voices, but some of the twentieth-century pieces require a larger ensemble because the parts divide.

Translations

Other volumes in the series have included singing translations. But the tendency now is to sing madrigals and partsongs in the original language. Since many of the settings are so closely tied to the sound and shape of the original words, we have instead provided a literal translation so that singers can understand what they are singing.

Editorial practice

The policy of the *Oxford Choral Classics* series is to use primary sources wherever possible (except for copyright pieces, which are reprinted as given by their original publishers). For the older material, primary sources, mostly printed, have been consulted wherever possible. In presenting our editions, the aim is first and foremost to serve the practical needs of non-specialist choirs. All material in square brackets is editorial. The comments below apply chiefly to the earlier material.

Prefatory staves have been given for pre-1700 sources, except when two parts are printed on one stave, when such information is added to the commentary. Note values have been reduced if necessary to give a crotchet pulse. Changes can be identified from the prefatory staves. Time signatures have been modernized. When there is a time change during a piece, the original is stated in the commentary. Key signatures are generally unchanged, including pieces notated in minor keys with one accidental too few. However, if transposition produces a key with one too many sharps, the correct modern signature has been used and the accidentals have been adjusted. Accidentals are expressed in the modern way and superfluous accidentals are omitted. Any doubts concerning the validity of original accidentals are mentioned in the commentary. Cautionary accidentals are added in round brackets, and these are also used for accidentals implied but not notated in the source. Editorial accidentals are in small print. In the figured bass of no. 40, the original convention of a sharp indicating a major chord and a flat a minor chord (with no naturals) has been retained. Spelling, punctuation, and capitalization have been modernized, though archaic words are retained and some early foreign texts that are familiar to singers in their original form have been only partially normalized. Final notes, when originally notated as longs or breves, are printed as a whole-bar note with pause. Early sources vary in the accuracy of the underlay; editorial interpretation of ambiguous placings has not always been noted. In sixteenth-and seventeenth-century editions, the exact repetition of the previous phrase is often shown by 'ij'. This is usually unambiguous (or at least no more ambiguous than the fully underlaid phrase), so we have not marked text added in accordance with the sign as editorial, though have noted in the commentary if there are any problems.

Obvious errors have been corrected without comment; cases of doubt or discrepancy are mentioned in the commentary. The length of the final notes of a phrase are often inconsistent; we have sometimes left them thus, as a reminder that in earlier music, the written length of a note may be a matter of convenience of notation rather than an instruction to the performer. Examples are in *Draw on, sweet Night*, no. 58, bar 115, and *Weep, weep mine eyes*, no. 59, bars 64–6. Beaming follows modern conventions, but slurs are not added merely to show underlay.

As regards compass, we have given the range of each part. Before 1700, the choice of voices was different and ranges were not necessarily suitable for modern SATB choirs. Some pieces were probably intended for ATTBarB, and even if trebles or sopranos were used on the top lines, it is likely that voices were not trained to sing as high as they are now. Alto parts tend to be low, but if the music is transposed up, tenor parts can become too high.

A convention of using two different sets of clefs grew up during the sixteenth century and declined in the seventeenth (see Commentary, p. 365, for explanation of notation):

a) (low clefs): C1, C3, C4, F4, as in no. 37 (Marenzio, *Scaldava il sol*),
b) (high clefs): G2, C2, C3, F3, as in no. 36 (Marenzio, *Crudel perché mi fuggi*).

These did not indicate different pitch levels, but were used for convenience of notation and to fit modal theory. Singers were not tied to any absolute pitch level, though the first (lower) clef combination probably was nearer modern pitch than the higher combination, which implied transposition down perhaps by a fourth or a fifth. We have generally left low-clef pieces at the original pitch or transposed them up a tone, but have transposed high-clef pieces down a tone or two (see, for example, the two Marenzio madrigals, nos. 36 and 37). The arrangement was less systematically followed in England; Morley, in his *A Plaine and Easie Introduction to Practicall Musicke* (1597), objected to it. In practice, he uses the two sets of clefs, but without consistently following the implied ranges. Modern singers may choose any pitch that suits them, though the higher the pitch, the more likely it is that the sopranos will sound shrill and the less likely it is that their words will be audible.

Bibliographical citations of the sources are as simple as possible, though with enough information to be able to identify them in the standard bibliographies and catalogues. Pieces taken from sixteenth-century printed anthologies are identified by their number in *RISM* (*Répertoire internationale des sources musicales*, specifically François Lesure, *Recueils imprimés, XVIe–XVIIe siècles*, G. Henle, Munich, 1960). The name of the composer is omitted and titles are generally given in short form, unless there is interesting information worth quoting. Capitalization is not retained for titles wholly or substantially in upper-case letters. Place and date of publication are given in modern form. The name of the publisher is included only for nineteenth- and twentieth-century music: most of the firms still survive.

Lute airs

We have included a selection of English lute airs. They have been neglected by vocal ensembles during the last few decades because of the belief that they were primarily intended for solo voice and lute, which is only partially true. Dowland's *Weep you no more, sad fountains* (no. 13) is an example that is far more effective with four voices. They present a practical problem, in that their tessitura is rather different from the madrigals of the time. The upper three parts tend to be higher (fine for sopranos and altos, but awkward for reluctant tenors), while the bass is too low for downwards transposition to help the tenor. In the original editions, these songs are printed with the soprano part and lute accompaniment on the left-hand page, so that a soprano can sing the melody and accompany herself on the lute (domestically, lutes were generally played by women); the other three parts were printed on the opposite page, facing outwards, so that they could be sung or played from the same copy. This permitted performance as a solo song, as a four-part vocal piece, or with a mixture of voices and instruments (probably viols), the latter two alternatives with or without lute. The difficulty of the singer or player who was taking the bottom part of the right-hand page getting near enough to the music if the soprano was playing the lute as well as singing makes it likely that when four parts were present, the lute would usually have been omitted. We have done so since, apart from that argument, lutenists prefer to play from editions or facsimiles of the original tablature, not from modern transcriptions. Facsimiles of the repertoire are published by Performers' Facsimiles and Brian Jordan Publications. Modern scores with tablature are published in *Musica Britannica*, vols. 6 (Dowland, but only the 2000 revised edition has tablature), 53, and 54.

Only the first verse of each song was underlaid, and sometimes it seems that the composers paid very little attention to how the subsequent verses fitted, especially in the lower parts. The worst example is Robert Jones's *Farewell, dear love* (no. 29). Singers and editors can break up or tie the original notes to get a satisfactory underlay, or else follow exactly the pattern of the first verse, adjusting only when a complete impasse is reached. We have preferred the latter, as being the way singers accustomed to dealing with 'ij' markings would have behaved.

Keyboard reductions

Keyboard reductions are given in their most readable and playable form, without always showing the movement of individual polyphonic voices, especially where these cross. This sometimes results in apparent parallel fifths and octaves, but we consider this preferable to the frequent sight of upstems and downstems crossed. Where all the voices of the texture are impossible to play, the keyboard reduction has been discreetly simplified. The marking of accidentals as editorial or cautionary is not carried through as pedantically as in the vocal parts. Keyboard reductions from the first editions of nineteenth- and twentieth-century works are not treated as sacrosanct and are amended without annotation.

Performance suggestions

We have given performance suggestions only in the keyboard reduction. Prescribing an initial tempo or mood is difficult since, apart from legitimate differences in understanding what the music is about, they can depend so much on circumstances, the size of the choir (or whether indeed there is more than one singer to a part), and the nature of the performance space. Fashions change, and generally the tempo of the earlier music in this collection is now taken faster than was considered normal a few decades ago. It is often helpful to take a section where the setting is syllabic in the basic note values of the piece (e.g. crotchets in no. 2), then think of the speed you would speak it in a fairly formal manner (without electronic aids) in the place where you intend to perform it. With large forces, however, tempi are likely to be slower. Dynamic suggestions have been added sparingly: solo ensembles will find it more interesting if dynamics emerge from their singing, while conductors will want to make their own decisions. Generally, in the earlier pieces, contrast is achieved within the phrase. Especially in Italian, but also in English and German madrigals in the Italian style, the stress of the words and the shaping of the phrase are all-important, and in polyphonic writing, these do not coincide. Climaxes are often built into the music when polyphonic writing becomes homophonic and by the harmonic movement. In a piece that is primarily contrapuntal, chordal sections should be special events, though not necessarily loud ones; see, for example, both parts of *Thule, the period of cosmography* (no. 57), where 'These things seem wondrous' is usually sung with quiet amazement. Barlines should not be allowed to dominate stress. Their presence is not, however, just a modern convenience: Renaissance singers would have been aware of the continuing *tactus* and would have realized that 'Vie più di posa' in no. 37, bar 37, made its effect by a rhythmic displacement. We have added pointers to performance style in the commentary to some of the pieces and have shown the groupings of three beats in duple contexts by square brackets above the accompaniment. The pattern $>\!\!\!=\!\!\!<\!\!\!=\!\!\!>$ is an attempt to show the *esclamazione*, an expressive way of singing a long chord with an initial accent then a rise from soft to a firm centre of the note and a fading at the end. For less dramatic long notes (especially final ones), the *messa di voce* is appropriate: just a crescendo and diminuendo from a quiet start.

We have avoided dynamic indications when several verses are underlaid to the same music. It is too easy to make loud and soft patterns in the more straightforward pieces too predictable: see the commentary to no. 41.

Acknowledgements

First, my thanks to John Rutter for enlisting my help in the series and swapping roles for this volume. His high standards with regard to all aspects of the work and his eager eye for detail are difficult to emulate. Brian Clark bore a considerable burden in checking sources and writing piano accompaniments, and his linguistic skills have been invaluable in understanding the words and producing the translations. As for all of this series and for my OUP *Messiah* edition, the typesetting has been done by Jenny Wilson with great skill and patience (especially with regard to reading my handwriting). Selene Mills kindly translated the *Lamento d'Arianna*. That Pearsall's *Lay a garland* is printed, probably for the first time, from the composer's manuscript, is due to help from Nicholas Temperley, Michael Pope, the Bristol Madrigal Society (which confirmed that it had no MSS), and Blaise Compton. I am grateful to Peter Branscombe for answering queries on the Haydn and Schubert pieces. At the final stage, Leofranc Holford-Strevens cast his expert eye over the translations. A more long-term debt is owed to all with whom I have sung the music.

The final stage of work on this volume coincides with the final days of my mother's life, so I dedicate it to her memory, with particular gratitude for her firm belief in the importance of education and the sacrifices she and my father made to ensure that I received the best that the British educational system could supply.

CLIFFORD BARTLETT

1. Dindirín, dindirín

Words: Anon.

ANON.
(*c*.1500)

37

rui - se - ñor,   Fác - teme a - ques - ta   em - ba - xa - ta."   Din - di - rin - dín.

carry this message for me.'   *Ding-a-ling.*

45

Din - di - rín,   din - di - rín,   din - di - rín - da - ña,   din - di - rin - dín.

51

3. "Rui - se - ñor, le rui - se - ñor,   Fác - teme a - ques - ta   em - ba - xa - ta

'Nightingale,   *carry this message for me.*

57

Y   dí - ga - lo a mon   a - mi   Que je   ya   só   ma - ri - ta - ta."

Tell my lover   *that I am now married.'*

65

Din - di - rin - dín.   Din - di - rín,   din - di - rín,   din - di - rín - da - ña,   din - di - rin - dín.

Ding-a-ling.

2. Il bianco e dolce cigno

Words by Giovanni Guidiccioni (1500–41)

JACQUES ARCADELT
(c.1507–68)

The white and sweet swan, dies singing,

and in tears

I reach the end of my life.

Strange and opposite fate,

that he dies disconsolate, *and I die happy.*

Death which in dying,   *fills me with joy and desire.*

If, in death, I feel no other pain   *I would be content to die*
a thousand times each day.

3. Of all the birds that I do know

Words by George Gascoigne (*c*.1534–77)

JOHN BARTLET
(*fl*. 1606–10)

1. Of all the birds that I do know Phil-ip my spar-row hath no peer; For sit she high, or sit she low, Be she far off, or be she near, There is no bird so fair, so fine, Nor yet so fresh as this of mine.

2. Come in a morn-ing mer-ri-ly, When Phil-ip hath been late-ly fed, Or in an eve-ning so-ber-ly, When Phil-ip list to go to bed, How she can chirp with mer-ry lip,

3. She ne-ver wand-ers far a-broad, But is at home when I do call, If I com-mand she lays on load, With lips, with teeth, with tongue and all She chants, she chirps, she makes such cheer, That I be-lieve she hath no peer;

For when she once hath felt a fit, Phil-ip will cry still:

yet, yet, yet, yet, yet, yet, yet, yet, yet, yet, yet, yet, yet, yet, yet, yet, yet. yet, yet,

4. And yet besides all this good sport,
My Philip can both sing and dance,
With new found toys of sundry sort,
My Philip can both prick and prance,
And if you say but 'fend cut, Phip',
Lord, how the peat will turn and skip,
For when . . .

5. And to tell truth he were to blame,
Having so fine a bird as she,
To make him all this goodly game,
Without suspect or jealousy;
He were a churl, and knew no good,
Would see her faint for lack of food;
For when . . .

4. All creatures now

Words: Anon.

JOHN BENNET
(*fl.* 1599–1614)

Then sang the shep - herds and nymphs of Di - a - na, nymphs

of Di - a - na: Long live fair O - ri - a - na,

5. Nachtwache No. 1

(from *Fünf Gesänge* Op. 104)

Words by Friedrich Rückert
(1788–1866)

JOHANNES BRAHMS
(1833–97)

Soft sounds from the breast,   *awakened by the breath of love,*

breathe out, trembling,

whether or not they open your ear,

may a loving heart open, and if none opens to you,

may a night breeze bear you, sighing, back to my heart.

6. The Evening Primrose

Words by John Clare (1793–1864)

BENJAMIN BRITTEN (1913–76)
Op. 47 no. 4

7. Never weather-beaten sail

Words by Thomas Campion

THOMAS CAMPION
(1557–1620)

SOPRANO (Cantus)

1. Ne - ver wea - ther-beat-en sail more will - ing bent to shore,
2. Ev - er bloom-ing are the joys of Heav'n's high Pa - ra - dise.

ALTO (Altus)

1. Ne - ver wea - ther-beat-en sail more will - ing bent to shore,
2. Ev - er bloom-ing are the joys of Heav'n's high Pa - ra - dise.

TENOR (Tenor)

1. Ne - ver wea - ther-beat-en sail more will - ing bent to shore,
2. Ev - er bloom-ing are the joys of Heav'n's high Pa - ra - dise.

BASS (Bassus)

1. Ne - ver wea - ther-beat-en sail more will - ing bent to shore,
2. Ev - er bloom-ing are the joys of Heav'n's high Pa - ra - dise.

Andante

(for rehearsal only)

5

Ne - ver tir - ed pil - grim's limbs af - fect - ed slum - ber more, Than my wea - ry
Cold age deafs not there our ears, nor va - pour dims our eyes; Glo - ry there the

Ne - ver tir - ed pil - grim's limbs af - fect - ed slum - ber more, Than my wea - ry
Cold age deafs not there our ears, nor va - pour dims our eyes; Glo - ry there the

Ne - ver tir - ed pil - grim's limbs af - fect - ed slum - ber more, Than my wea - ry
Cold age deafs not there our ears, nor va - pour dims our eyes; Glo - ry there the

Ne - ver tir - ed pil - grim's limbs af - fect - ed slum - ber more, Than my wea - ry
Cold age deafs not there our ears, nor va - pour dims our eyes; Glo - ry there the

8. So weich und warm

Words by Paul Heyse
(1830–1914)

PETER CORNELIUS
(1824–74)

No arm embraces you more gently and warmly   *than when your*

mother cuddles you,   *no comfort is as familiar to you*

as her eyes resting upon you.

Therefore try to behave like a good child   *so that,*

when she dies, she can bless you: otherwise, even if love and friendship should remain,

you will yet

most of all it will make you happy   _that you were_

your mother's child.   _Therefore_

try to behave like a good child   so that,   when she dies, she can bless you:

otherwise, even if love and friendship remained,

you would be alone without your mother's soul.

9. Trois chansons de Charles d'Orléans

Words by Charles d'Orléans
(1394–1465)

CLAUDE DEBUSSY
(1862–1918)
edited by John Rutter

I. Dieu! qu'il la fait bon regarder!

Lord! how fair she is to see . . .

This gracious, good, and beauteous lady;

For all the great virtues which are in her   *everyone is ready to praise her.*

Who could tire of her?   *Her beauty*

-jours sa beau - té re - nou - vel - le. Dieu! qu'il la fait bon re - gar -

Tous - jours sa beau - té re-nou-vel - le. Dieu qu'il la fait bon re-gar-

-jours sa beau - té re - nou - vel - le. re -

-jours sa beau - té re - nou - vel - le.

always renews itself. *Lord! how fair she is to see . . .*

- der, La gra - ci - eu - se bonne et bel - le!

- der, La gra - ci - eu - se bonne et bel - le!

-gar - der, La gra - ci - eu - se bonne et bel - le!

La gra - ci - eu - se bonne et bel - le!

this gracious, good and beauteous lady!

On neither side of the sea . . .   do I know any lady or maiden . . .

who is so perfect in all virtues.   It is a dream

Bar 18: All voices have an erroneous comma after 'de là' in the MS and 1910 sources.

even to think about her: *Lord! how fair she is to see!*

II. Quant j'ai ouy le tabourin

When I heard the drum sounding, to call everyone to the May festivities . . .

*See Commentary.

† Or ♩ ♪♪♪, to be consistent with bars 23 and 42.

As I lay in bed I was not disturbed . . .

nor lifted my head from the pillow;

I said: . . .   *'It is too early in the morning,*

I shall go back to sleep for a little:'

Let the young people share out their prizes [from the festivities];

Très modéré
doux et expressif

non-cha-loir _____ m'ac-coin-te-ray A lui _____ je m'a-bu-ti-ne-

pp (à bouche fermée) *

pp (à bouche fermée) *

la   la la la la   la   la la la la   la   la la la   la la   la   la la la   la la la   la la

pp doux et expressif

la _____   la _____

Très modéré

pp doux et expressif

con Ped.

Coolness will be my friend and companion;

-ray   Trou-vé   l'ay   plus prou-chain voi-sin;

1st ALTOS
pp (à bouche fermée) *

la   la la la la   la   la la la la   la   la la la   la la   la la la   la la la   la la

la _____   la _____

I have found him to be closer to me [than other people's company].

* 'with mouth closed', i.e. humming.

* This instruction to hum (found in the 1910 edition only) is incompatible with the 'a' sound (originally in the manuscript but still remaining, probably through an oversight, in the 1910 edition). It is suggested that the 'a' be disregarded.

† In the MS and the 1908 edition the last four bars of B2 are as follows:

III. Yver, vous n'estes qu'un villain

Winter, you're nothing but a wretch;

Summer is pleasant and gracious . . .

as its heralds, April and May, bear witness with every evening

and morning.

Summer clothes the fields, woods, and flowers . . .

Bar 20, bass: the second note of the bar is B in the MS and published editions, but A seems more likely.

in its livery of green . . . *and many other colours . . .*

by nature's command. *But you,*

Winter,   are too full of snow,

rain, wind, and sleet.

You should have been banished into exile.

Without any flattery, I shall speak my mind:

Winter, you're nothing but a wretch.

* 'in strict time, without hurrying'

10. To be sung of a summer night on the water

Two unaccompanied partsongs

FREDERICK DELIUS (1862–1934)
edited by John Rutter

I

* Sing on vowel 'uh' (as in 'love'), with a very loose mouth (almost closed in the *pianissimo*)
which should be gradually opened or shut accordingly as more or less tone is wanted. Breath
should be taken only at the sign ' if possible, quietly and quickly in order to preserve the *legato*. [F.D.]

** ⌐ ¬ = slightly prominent.

II

* See note on performance, p. 62.   ** Bracketed sections of the solo part could be omitted. [Ed.]

* If soloist is omitting bracketed sections, he should sing the small note in this bar, then rest for three beats. [Ed.]

* The solo voice should sing to syllables as indicated, introducing delicate *staccati* at appropriate places (which are generally where the syllable 'luh' is put). On *staccato* notes the vowel should be sung for a very short time and the remainder of the notes continued on the sound of 'l'.

The accompanying voices should sing on 'uh' (as in 'love'). A slight aspirate, without taking the voice off before it, may be made at (*i*) all repeated notes and (*ii*) the first notes of slurs (unless it happens to come after a breath, in which case the aspirate is best omitted). [F.D.]

11. Come, heavy sleep

Words: Anon.

JOHN DOWLAND
(1563–1626)

12. Can she excuse my wrongs

Words: Anon.

JOHN DOWLAND
(1563–1626)

13. Weep you no more, sad fountains

Words: Anon.

JOHN DOWLAND
(1563–1626)

14. As torrents in summer

Words by Henry Longfellow
(1807–82)

EDWARD ELGAR (1857–1934)
from Op. 30

15. My love dwelt in a Northern land
Romance

Words by Andrew Lang
(1844–1912)

EDWARD ELGAR (1857–1934)
Op. 18 no. 3

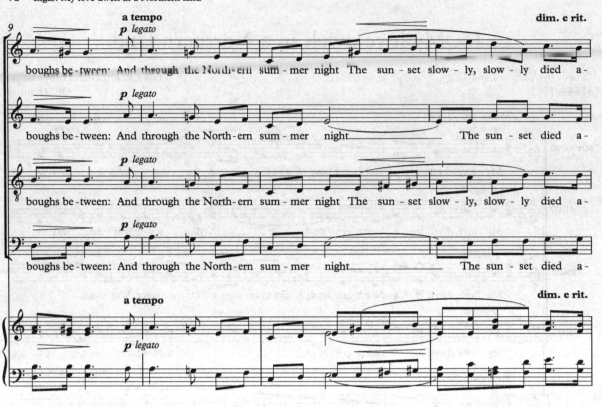

* The passages of vocal accompaniment to be sung as softly and smoothly as possible and without accent.

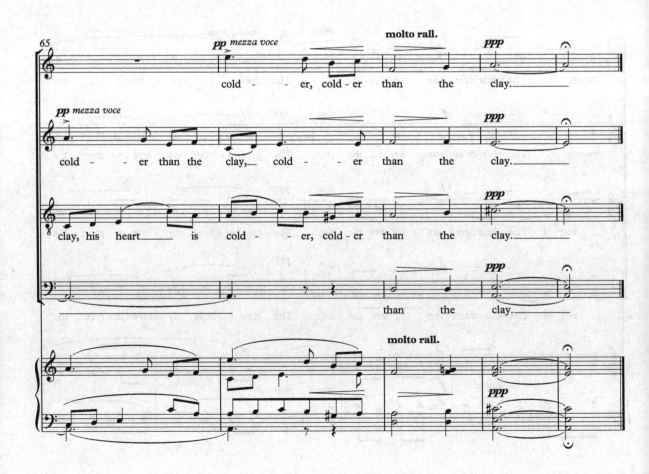

16. There is sweet music

Words by Alfred, Lord Tennyson (1809–92)

EDWARD ELGAR (1857–1934)
Op. 53 no. 1

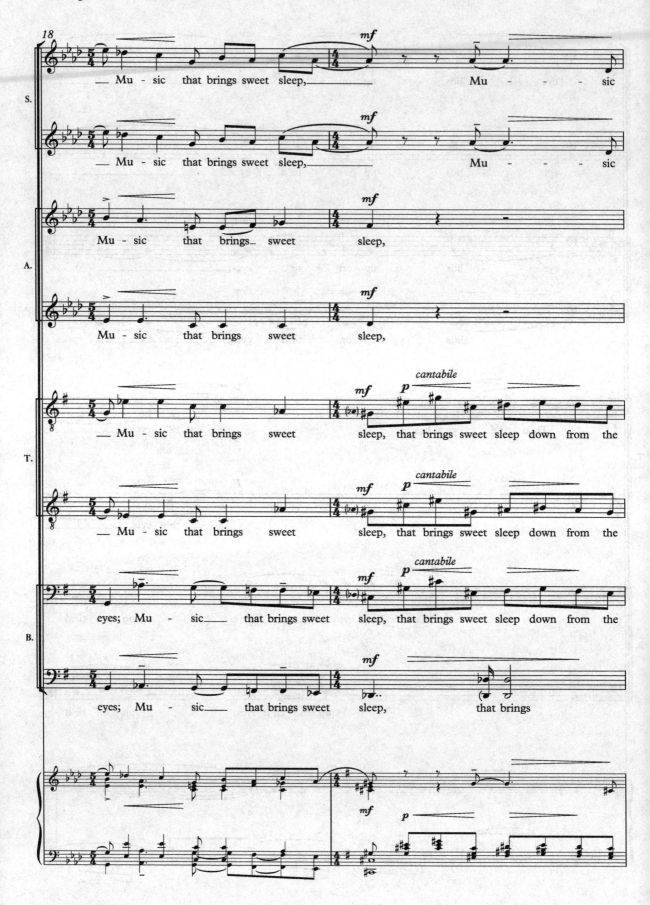

Rome, Dec. 1907

17. Fair Phyllis I saw sitting all alone

Words: Anon.

JOHN FARMER
(*fl.* 1591–1601)

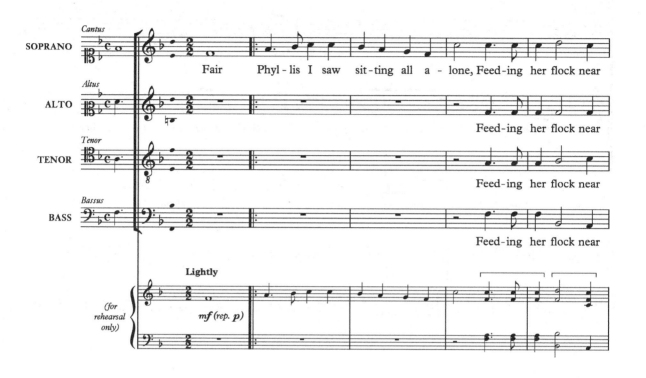

18. My spirit sang all day

Words by Robert Bridges
(1844–1930)

GERALD FINZI (1901–56)
Op. 17 no. 1

jea-lous ears grew whist; O my joy Mu - sic from hea - ven is't,___ Sent___

Mu - sic from hea - ven is't,___

___ for our joy? She al - so came and heard; O my joy, What, said she, is this

Sent for our joy?

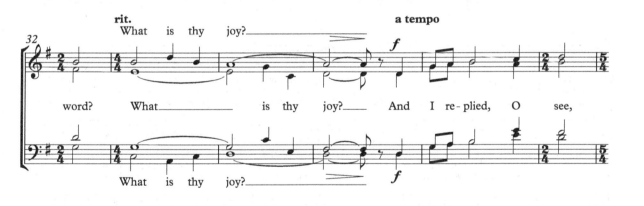

rit.   What is thy joy?___   **a tempo**

word? What___ is thy joy?___ And I re - plied, O see,

What is thy joy?___

allargando

O my joy,___ 'Tis thee, I cried, 'tis thee:___ Thou___ art my joy.___

19. Since first I saw your face

Words. Anon.

THOMAS FORD
(d. 1648)

May be sung a tone higher.

20. Lieto godea

Words: Anon.

GIOVANNI GABRIELI
(*c*.1555–1612)

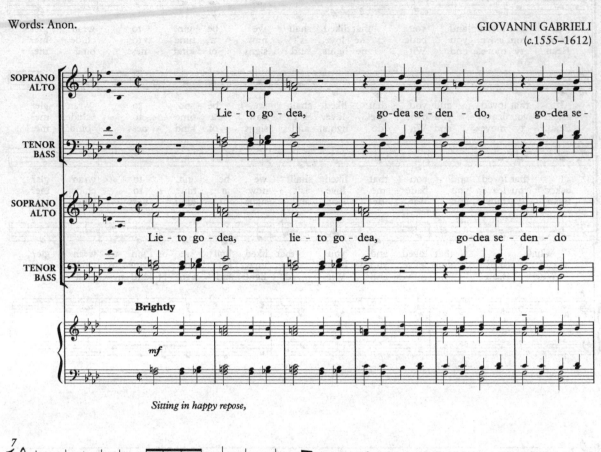

Sitting in happy repose,

enjoying April's sweetly trembling breezes.

Every creature sighed of love all the time

With a mortal dart   Love came flying and pierced my heart;

Alas!

he took flight: woe is me!

Thus I shall have

21. Amor vittorioso

Tutti venite armati

Words: Anon.

GIOVANNI GASTOLDI
(c.1554–1609)

1. Everyone come armed,
2. They seem strong heroes

O my strong soldiers.
those who are against you.

Both sections of each verse are repeated.

1. *I am the invincible*   *skilful archer.*   *Do not be afraid,*
2. *Those who might hurt you*   *do not know how.*   *Do not be afraid,*

but joined in a perfect formation   *follow me boldly.*
be courageous and strong,   *be smart in battle.*

3. Happily now move your feet, *let the prizes be yours,*
4. Already he lies dead on the ground *who had waged war against us,*

Now let us beat scorn away,
Now all his other followers

for it does not deserve to live.   *Do not be afraid,*   *the glory will be everlasting*
let us boldly crush.   *Do not be afraid,*   *look how those who aren't dead*

and victory is assured.
are running away, already scattered and defeated.

22. Ah, dear heart

Words: Anon.

ORLANDO GIBBONS
(1583–1625)

23. The silver swan

Words: Anon.

ORLANDO GIBBONS
(1583–1625)

24. What is our life?

Words by Sir Walter Raleigh (?1552–1618)

ORLANDO GIBBONS
(1583–1625)

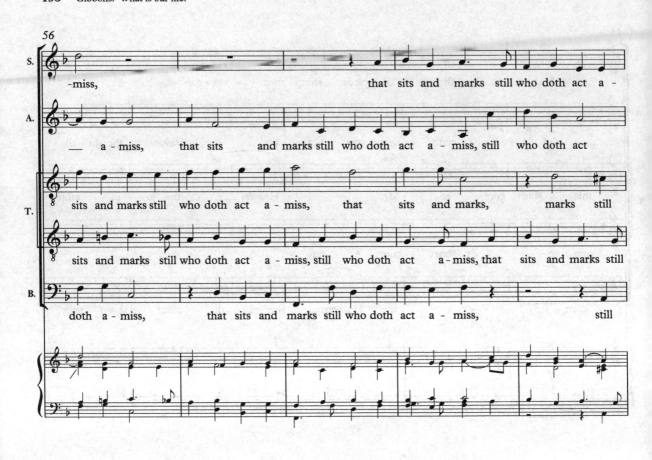

25. Tanzen und springen

Gagliarda

Words. Anon.

HANS LEO HASSLER
(1564–1612)

1. *Dancing and leaping,*   *singing and playing;*
2. *Beautiful maidens, in green meadows,*

1. *lutes and violins should also not be silent,*
2. *strolling,*   *and chatting,*

music-making

and celebrating

fills my mind.

joking with friends,

warms my heart more

than silver and gold.

26. Ach, Weh des Leiden

Words: Anon.

HANS LEO HASSLER
(1564–1612)

Ah, woe and grief,   must we then part?

Ah, woe to poor me, who would not pity me?

Ah, the woe of pain, *which I feel in my heart.*

Must I then give you up?

It will cost me my life!

27. Die Harmonie in der Ehe

(Matrimonial harmony)

Words by Johann Nikolaus Götz (18th c.)

JOSEPH HAYDN
(1732–1809)

Oh, wonderful harmony!   *What he wants, she wants too,*

he likes a drink, she too,   *he likes playing l'hombre, she too,*   *he likes the purse, and likes to play the lord and master,*

that's her custom, too.

-brauch. Sie hat den Beu - tel gern und spie - let gern den Herrn, auch
-brauch. Sie hat den Beu - tel gern und spie - let gern den Herrn, auch
-brauch. Er hat den Beu - tel gern und spie - let gern den Herrn, auch das ist sein Ge-
-brauch. Er hat den Beu - tel gern und spie - let gern den Herrn, auch das ist sein Ge-

das ist ihr Ge-brauch, ist ihr Ge-brauch. O wun-der-ba-re
das ist ihr Ge-brauch, ist ihr Ge-brauch. O wun-der-ba-re Har -
-brauch, ist sein Ge-brauch. O wun-der-ba-re Har - mo-nie, was
-brauch, ist sein Ge-brauch. O wun-der-ba-re Har - mo-nie, o wun-der-ba-re

28. Innsbruck, ich muss dich lassen

Words: Anon.

HEINRICH ISAAC
(*c.*1450–1517)

1. Innsbruck, I must leave you,
3. My comfort above all women,

I am going on my way,
I will be yours forever,

to a foreign land.
always true, preserve your honour.

My joy has been taken from me
Now God must protect you

which I cannot regain
and keep you in all virtue

since I am suffering.
until I return.

2. I must now bear great suffering,   that I alone shall bemoan

to my dearest loved one.   Ah dear, let me, poor man,

feel mercy for you in my heart,

for I must be away.

29. Farewell, dear love

Words: Anon.

ROBERT JONES
(*fl.* 1597–1615)

SOPRANO
Cantus

1. Fare - well, dear love, since thou wilt needs be gone,
2. Fare - well, fare - well, since this I find is true,
3. Ten thou - sand times fare - well! Yet stay a - while!

ALTO
Altus

1. Fare - well, dear love, since thou wilt needs be gone,
2. Fare - well, fare - well, since this I find is true,
3. Ten thou - sand times fare - well! Yet stay a - while!

TENOR
Tenor

1. Fare - well, dear love, since thou wilt needs be gone,
2. Fare - well, fare - well, since this I find is true,
3. Ten thou - sand times fare - well! Yet stay a - while!

BASS
Bassus

1. Fare - well, dear love, since thou wilt needs be gone,
2. Fare - well, fare - well, since this I find is true,
3. Ten thou - sand times fare - well! Yet stay a - while!

Flowing

(for rehearsal only)

Mine eyes do show my life is al - most done. Yet I will ne - ver die
I will not spend more time in woo - ing you. But I will seek else - where,
Sweet, kiss me once, sweet kiss - es time be - guile. I have no power to move.

So long as I can spy.
If I may find her there.
How now, am I in love?

There be ma-ny moe,
Shall I bid her go?
Wilt thou needs be gone?

Though that she do
What and if I
Go then, all is

So long as I can spy.
If I may find her there.
How now, am I in love?

There be ma-ny moe,
Shall I bid her go?
Wilt thou needs be gone?

Though that she do go,
What and if I do?
Go then, all is one.

So long as I can spy.
If I may find her there.
How now, am I in love?

There be ma-ny moe,
Shall I bid her go?
Wilt thou needs be gone?

Though that she do go,
What and if I do?
Go then, all is one.

So long as I can spy.
If I may find her there.
How now, am I in love?

There be ma-ny moe,
Shall I bid her go?
Wilt thou needs be gone?

Though that she do go,
What and if I do?
Go then, all is one.

go,
do?
one.

There be ma-ny moe, I fear not, Why, then let her go, I care not.
Shall I bid her go, and spare not? O no, no, no, no, I dare not.
Wilt thou needs be gone? O hie thee! Nay, stay, and do no more de-ny me.

There be ma-ny moe, I fear not, Why, then let her go, I care not.
Shall I bid her go, and spare not? O no, no, no, no, I dare not.
Wilt thou needs be gone? O hie thee! Nay, stay, and do no more de-ny me.

There be ma-ny moe, I fear not, Why, then let her go, I care not.
Shall I bid her go, and spare not? O no, no, no, no, I dare not.
Wilt thou needs be gone? O hie thee! Nay, stay, and do no more de-ny me.

There be ma-ny moe, I fear, I fear not, Why, then let her go, I care not.
Shall I bid her go, and spare, and spare not? O no, no, no, no, I dare not.
Wilt thou needs be gone? O hie, O hie thee! Nay, stay, and do no more de-ny me.

30. Mille regrets

Words by Jean Lemaire de Belges (*c.*1473– after 1513)

JOSQUIN DES PREZ
(*c.*1450/55–1521)

A thousand regrets at leaving you

and putting your lovely face at a distance.

I suffer such deep sorrow and grievous pain

that I will soon be seen to end my days.

31. Chi chi li chi

Words. Anon.

ORLANDE DE LASSUS
(1532–94)

Go to hell, I'm no longer in love.

You slept all night,   *You never kissed me.*

Take your bagpipes!   *Go and play wherever you like!*

*Play if you want to play!**

★ See commentary

Stop – you're bursting my ears!   Stop, Martin!   Stop, Lucia!

Oh, my lady,   may you grow a beard,

May you come to a sticky end!   *Play, and don't give up.*

Lift your leg, Lady Lucia,   hold out your hand,   take the bagpipes,

dance a little with master Martin.

32. La nuit froide et sombre

Words by Joachim du Bellay (1522–60)

ORLANDE DE LASSUS
(1532–94)

May be sung a tone higher.

sleep, as sweet as honey, on the eyes.

Then day, following   and leading men to toil,

spreads its light,   and with varying colours

weaves and ordains this great universe.

* Upper note is an editorial alternative.

33. Bonjour mon cœur

Words by Pierre de Ronsard (1524–85)

ORLANDE DE LASSUS
(1532–94)

my sparrow,   my gentle turtle-dove,   good-day, my sweet wild bird.

34. Matona, mia cara

Words: Anon.

ORLANDE DE LASSUS
(1532–1594)

My dear Lady, *I'd love to sing*

a song below your window

I'm a lancer, and a good lad.

Ti pre-go m'a-scol - ta - re,   Che mi can-tar de bon,

Ti pre-go m'a-scol - ta-re, Che mi can - tar de bon,

Ti pre-go m'a-scol - ta - re, Che mi can - tar de bon,

Ti pre-go m'a-scol - ta - re,   Che mi can - tar de bon,

f

Please listen to me,   for I sing well,

E mi ti fol - ler be - ne,   Co - me gre - co e   ca - pon. Don don

E mi ti fol - ler be - ne,   Co - me   gre-co e ca - pon. Don don

E mi ti fol - ler be - ne, Co - me gre - co e ca - pon. Don don

E mi ti fol - ler be - ne,   Co - me gre - co e   ca - pon. Don don

mp

and I love you greatly,   as a Greek does his capon.

When I go hunting,   *hunting with a falcon,*

I'll bring you woodcocks as fat as a kidney.

Though I do not know so many elegant phrases,

and know nothing of Petrarch, *or the fountain of Helicon,*

35. Revoici venir du printemps

Words by Jean-Antoine de Baïf (1532–89)

CLAUDE LE JEUNE
(1528/30–1600)

Here comes the spring again,   the beautiful

season of love.

The *rechants* may be sung by choir, alternating with soloists or semichorus singing the *chants*.

Chant à 2

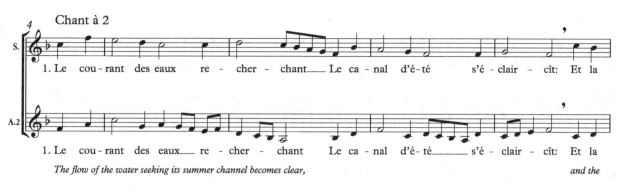

1. Le cou-rant des eaux re - cher - chant___ Le ca-nal d'é-té s'é-clair - cît: Et la

1. Le cou-rant des eaux___ re - cher - chant Le ca-nal d'é-té___ s'é - clair - cît: Et la

The flow of the water seeking its summer channel becomes clear,   *and the*

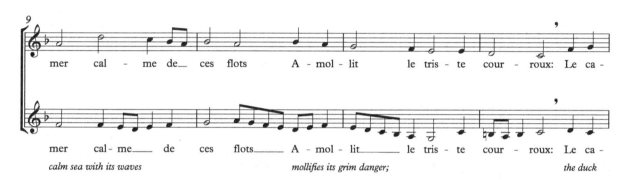

mer cal - me de___ ces flots A - mol - lit le tris - te cour - roux: Le ca-

mer cal - me___ de ces flots___ A - mol - lit___ le tris - te cour - roux: Le ca-

calm sea with its waves   *mollifies its grim danger;*   *the duck*

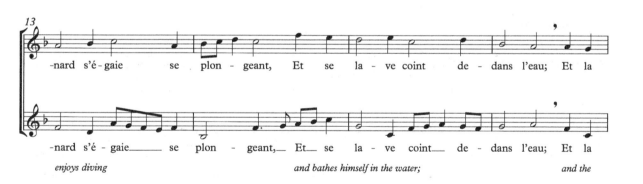

-nard s'é-gaie se plon - geant, Et se la - ve coint de - dans l'eau; Et la

-nard s'é-gaie___ se plon - geant,___ Et se la - ve coint___ de - dans l'eau; Et la

enjoys diving   *and bathes himself in the water;*   *and the*

grue___ qui four - che___ son vol Re-tra - ver - se l'air___ et s'en___ va.

grue___ qui four - che son vol Re-tra - ver - se___ l'air et___ s'en va.

crane, which forks its wing,   *criss-crosses the sky and goes away.*

Rechant à 5

Re-voi - ci ve - nir du prin - temps, L'a-mou - reu - se et bel - le sai - son.

mf

Chant à 3

2. Le so - leil é - clai - re lui - sant___ D'u-ne plus se - rei - ne clar - té: Du nu -

The sun shines   *with brightness more serene;*   *it chases*

-a - ge l'om - bre s'en - fuit,___ Qui_ se joue et_ court et_ noir - cit Et fo - rêts et champs et

shadows from the clouds   *which play and run and darken*   *the forests and fields and hills.*

cou-teaux. Le la - beur hu-main re - ver - dit, Et la pré dé - cou - vre ses fleurs.

cou-teaux. Le la - beur hu-main re - ver - dit, Et la pré dé - cou - vre ses fleurs.

The fields that men work become green   and the meadow reveals its flowers.

Rechant à 5

S. Re-voi - ci ve-nir du prin - temps, L'a-mou - reu - se et bel - le sai - son.

A. Re-voi - ci ve-nir du prin - temps, L'a-mou - reu - se et bel - le sai - son.

Re-voi - ci ve-nir du prin - temps, L'a-mou - reu - se et bel - le sai - son.

T. Re-voi - ci ve-nir du prin - temps, L'a-mou - reu - se et bel - le sai - son.

B. Re-voi - ci ve-nir du prin - temps, L'a-mou - reu - se et bel - le sai - son.

mf

Venus' son, Cupid,   sowing the world with his arrows,

will inflame with his fire   *creatures that fly in the air,*   *creatures*

that crawl in the fields,   *creatures that swim in water.*   *Even the being*

with no sensation   *will feel love and drown in pleasure.*

Rechant à 5

Chant à 5

Let us laugh too,   *and let us seek the revels and games of spring:*   *everything*

laughs with pleasure: *let us celebrate the merry season.*

Rechant à 5

36. Crudel perche mi fuggi

(Unkind, oh stay thy flying)

Words by G. B. Guarini (1538–1612)
English text by Thomas Watson (1557–92)

LUCA MARENZIO
(1553/4–99)

Ah, cruel!   why do you flee from me   If you desire my death so much?

You alone are my heart

Do you think by fleeing,

Cruel one, that you will make me die?

Ah, one cannot die

without pain

and one who has no heart can feel no pain.

37. Scaldava il sol

Words by Luigi Alamanni (1495–1556)

LUCA MARENZIO
(1553/4–99)

As the midday sun was scorching

the arch of the lion's back,

in his favourite resting-place,

under the bush   laden with most branches,

the shepherd was sleeping there

with his sheep nearby;   *the peasant was stretched out,*

released from his toil,   *greedier for rest*

than for corn;   *the birds,*

wild beasts,   every human being sought the shade

and fell silent;   only the cicada

did not feel at peace.

38. O Mirtillo, Mirtillo, anima mia

Words by G. B. Guarini
(1538–1612)

CLAUDIO MONTEVERDI
(1567–1643)

O Mirtillo, Mirtillo my love,

if you see here within me   *how stands the heart of her*

whom you call

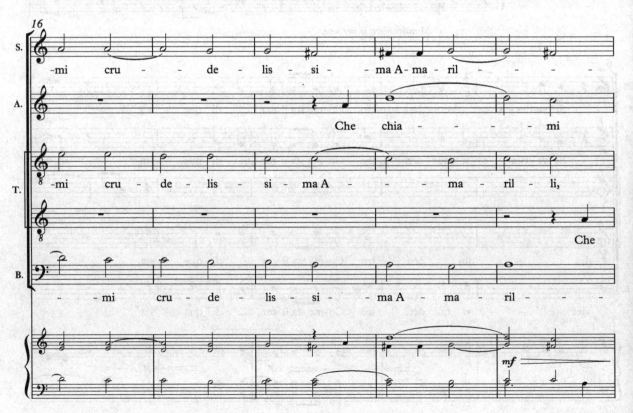

the most cruel Amarilli,

I am sure that you would

feel for her   that pity which instead you ask from her.

O souls too unhappy in love!

What use is it to you, my heart, to be loved?

What use is it to me to have so dear a lover?

Why, cruel fate, do you separate us ... *when love*

has united us? ... *And you, why do you unite us* ... *if fate separates us,*

perfidious love?

39. Ohimè se tanto amate

Words by G. B. Guarini
(1538–1612)

CLAUDIO MONTEVERDI
(1567–1643)

if you love so much to hear me say, 'alas',

why do you make

the one who says it die?   *If I die*

you will be able to hear only one weary and sad 'alas!'

But if, my love,

you want to give me life,

then you shall have   *thousands and thousands of sweet sighs.*

40. Lamento d'Arianna

I. Lasciatemi morire

Words by
Ottavio Rinuccini (1562–1621)

CLAUDIO MONTEVERDI
(1567–1643)

Leave me to die;

whom do you

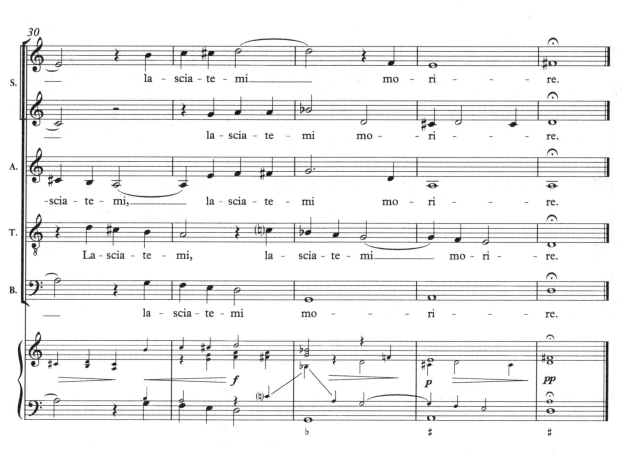

II. O Teseo, Teseo mio

O Theseus, O my Theseus,

Yes, I will call you mine, for you are truly mine,

although you vanish (ah, cruel!) from my eyes,

turn back,

26

S. — gi - ti, Te - seo mi - o,   vol - gi - ti,

Vol - gi - ti, Te -

A. — gi - ti, Te - seo mi - o,   vol - gi - ti Te -

T. Te - seo mi - o, vol - gi - ti Te - seo,

B. Te - seo mi - o,   vol - gi - ti, Te -

my Theseus,

31

S. Te - seo, O Di - o!

-seo, O Di - o! Vol - gi - ti in - die -

A. -seo, O Di - o!

T. O Di - o! Vol - gi - ti in - die - tro a ri - mi-

B. - seo, O Di - o! Vol - gi - ti in - die - tro a ri - mi-

f   mf

(O God!)   *turn back to gaze again at her*

who left for you her homeland and kingdom,

and now on these sands,

food for pitiless and cruel beasts,

will leave her bare bones.

O Theseus, O my Theseus,

if you knew, O God!

if you knew (alas!) how troubled is

But with gentle breezes you happily depart   *and I lament here;*

for you Athens prepares joyful, proud pomp,

* If sung chorally, Tenors should divide for bars 84–89 and the Alto part be sung by 1st Tenors.

will joyfully embrace,   and I shall never see you again,

O mother, O my father.

III. Dove, dove è la fede

Where, where is the faith   *you swore so often to me?*

Is it thus that you seat me on the high throne

of your forefathers?   *Are these the crowns*

with which you adorn my hair?   Are these the sceptres,

these the gems and jewels?   Do you leave me abandoned

for beasts to tear and devour me?

Ah Theseus,

IV. Ahi, che non pur risponde!

Ah, he still does not answer!   *Ah, he is deafer than an asp*

to my laments!   *O storms, O tempests, O winds, submerge him*

[all off] you beneath these waves! Hurry, sea monsters and whales,

and with his unclean limbs fill the deep whirlpools.

What am I saying, *(alas!) what am I raving about?* *Wretched, alas,*

what am I asking? *O Theseus,* *O my Theseus,*

it was not I

who uttered such fierce words:

my distress spoke,   my pain spoke;   my tongue did speak, yes,

but certainly not my heart.

41. My bonny lass she smileth

Words: Anon.

THOMAS MORLEY
(1557/8–1602)

42. Now is the month of maying

Words: Anon.

THOMAS MORLEY
(1557/8–1602)

43. Music, when soft voices die

Words by P. B. Shelley
(1792–1822)

C. HUBERT H. PARRY
(1848–1918)

44. Il est bel et bon

Words: Anon.

PIERRE PASSEREAU
(*fl.* 1509–47)

My husband's a handsome good fellow, dear.

There were two country women,   and one said to the other: 'you have a good
                                                                                    husband.'

He doesn't annoy me, he doesn't

beat me either.

He does the cleaning,

He feeds the chickens,   *and I take my pleasure.*

Doesn't it make you laugh, dear,   *when the*

45. Lay a garland

Words from Beaumont and Fletcher

ROBERT PEARSALL
(1795–1856)

46. Rest, sweet nymphs

Words: Anon.

FRANCIS PILKINGTON
(c.1570–1638)

47. Ancor che col partire

Words attrib. Alfonso d'Avalos
(1502–46)

CIPRIANO DE RORE
(c.1515–65)

Although in leaving

I feel myself dying,　　　　　　　　*I would like to leave every moment,*

every moment,   such is the pleasure I feel

of a life gained in returning;

thus, a thousand times each day

I would love to leave you,

so sweet are my returns.

48. Douce mémoire

Words by François I (1494–1547)

PIERRE SANDRIN
(*c.*1490 – after 1561)

Sweet memory, consummated in pleasure,

O happy age,

which brings such understanding,   the constancy of us two so loving.

Which knew so well how to overpower our ills,

has now lost its power,   *breaking the*

but de ma seule e-spé-ran-ce, Ser-vant d'ex-em-ple à tous pi-

but de ma seule e-spé-ran - ce, Ser-vant d'ex-em-ple à tous_____ pi-

but de ma seule e - spé-ran - ce, Ser - vant d'ex - em - ple à tous pi-

but de ma seule e - spé-ran - ce, Ser - vant d'ex - em - ple à tous pi-

dim.

object of my only hope, *making an example piteous for all to see.*

-teux à voir. Fi - ni_____ le bien, le mal sou-dain com-

-teux à voir._____ Fi - ni le bien, le mal sou - dain_____

-teux à voir. Fi - ni le bien, le mal sou - dain com-

-teux à voir. Fi - ni_____ le bien, le mal sou-

cresc. *mf*

Good is finished, *the bad suddenly begins.*

49. Der Tanz

Words: Kolumban Schnitzer von Meerau

FRANZ SCHUBERT
(1797–1828)

1. Es redet und träumet die Jugend so viel von Tanzen, Galoppen, Ge-
2. Jüngst wähnt' auch ein Fräulein mit trübem Gefühl, schon hätte ihr Stündlein ge-

1. *Youth talks and dreams so much* ... *of dances, galops, and parties;*
2. *Recently a girl thought, in her sadness,* ... *that her last hour had come.*

-la - gen, auf ein - mal er - reicht sie ein trüg - li - ches Ziel, da

-schla - gen. Doch stand noch das Räd - chen der Par - ze nicht still, nun

suddenly it reaches a false goal,   *then*
But the wheel of fate did not stand still,   *now*

hört man sie seuf - zen und kla - gen.   Bald
schö - ner die Freu - den ihr ta - gen.   Drum

we hear it sigh and complain.   *Soon*
joys are dawning for her more beautifully.   *So*

schmer - zet der Hals, und bald schmer - zet die Brust, ver - schwun - den ist al - le die
Freun - de, er - he - bet den fro - hen Ge - sang, es le - be die teu - re I -

the throat hurts, and soon the chest hurts,   *lost is the heavenly delight.*
friends raise the joyous song: *'May dear Irene live long, to be sure,*

'Just this time, health, come back to me!'   *thus*
may she often think of false Fate,   *but*

pleads from heaven the hopeful glance.
may her cheerful gaze never grow sad.'

50. Ach Elslein, liebes Elselein

Words. Anon.

LUDWIG SENFL
(c.1486 – c.1543)

1. Oh Elsie,   my dear little Elsie,   how happy
2. That causes me   great pain   my dearest
3. I hope time   will end it,   I hope luck

I'd be with you;   there are two deep rivers
darling;   I speak with all my heart,
will return,   and everything will turn out well,

© Oxford University Press 2001. Photocopying copyright material is illegal.

between you and me.
that it's a great misfortune.
dearest little Elsie.

51. Au joli bois

Words: Anon.

CLAUDIN DE SERMISY
(c.1490–1562)

To the pretty wood   overshadowed by care,

I must go   to endure my sadness.   Full of

sorrow from a numbing memory, *I must eat many choke-pears.*

In a garden filled with black flowers,

from both my eyes come sobs and tears.   *Fie to jollity*

and boldness!   *Regret oppresses me, since I have lost my love.*

Alas, how I suffer, time presses hard on me,

I assure you: solace, you have no more currency.

52. The blue bird

Words by Mary Coleridge (1861–1907)

C. V. STANFORD (1852–1924)
Op. 119 no. 3

53. Heraclitus

Words by CALLIMACHUS (*c.*320–*c.*240 BC)
Translated by William Cory (1823–89)

C. V. STANFORD (1852–1924)
Op. 110 no. 4

of - ten you and I Had tired the sun with talk-ing and sent him down the sky. And

How of - ten you and I Had tired the sun with talk - ing and sent him down the sky. And

How of - ten you and I Had tired the sun with talk - ing and sent him down the sky. And

How of - ten you and I Had tired the sun with talk - ing and sent him down the sky. And

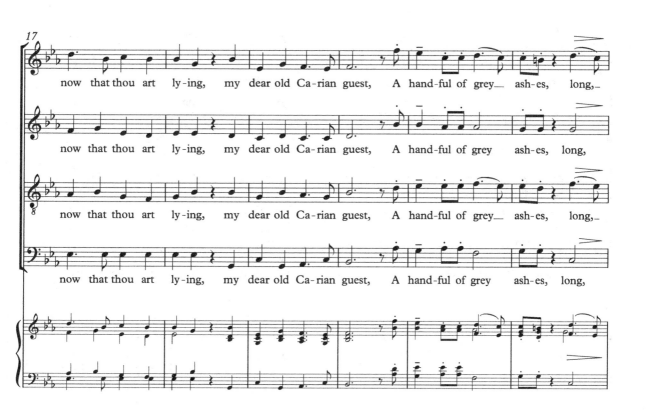

now that thou art ly - ing, my dear old Ca-rian guest, A hand-ful of grey— ash-es, long,—

now that thou art ly - ing, my dear old Ca-rian guest, A hand-ful of grey ash-es, long,

now that thou art ly - ing, my dear old Ca-rian guest, A hand-ful of grey— ash-es, long,—

now that thou art ly - ing, my dear old Ca-rian guest, A hand-ful of grey ash-es, long,

54. The long day closes

Words by Henry Chorley
(1808–72)

ARTHUR SULLIVAN
(1842–1900)

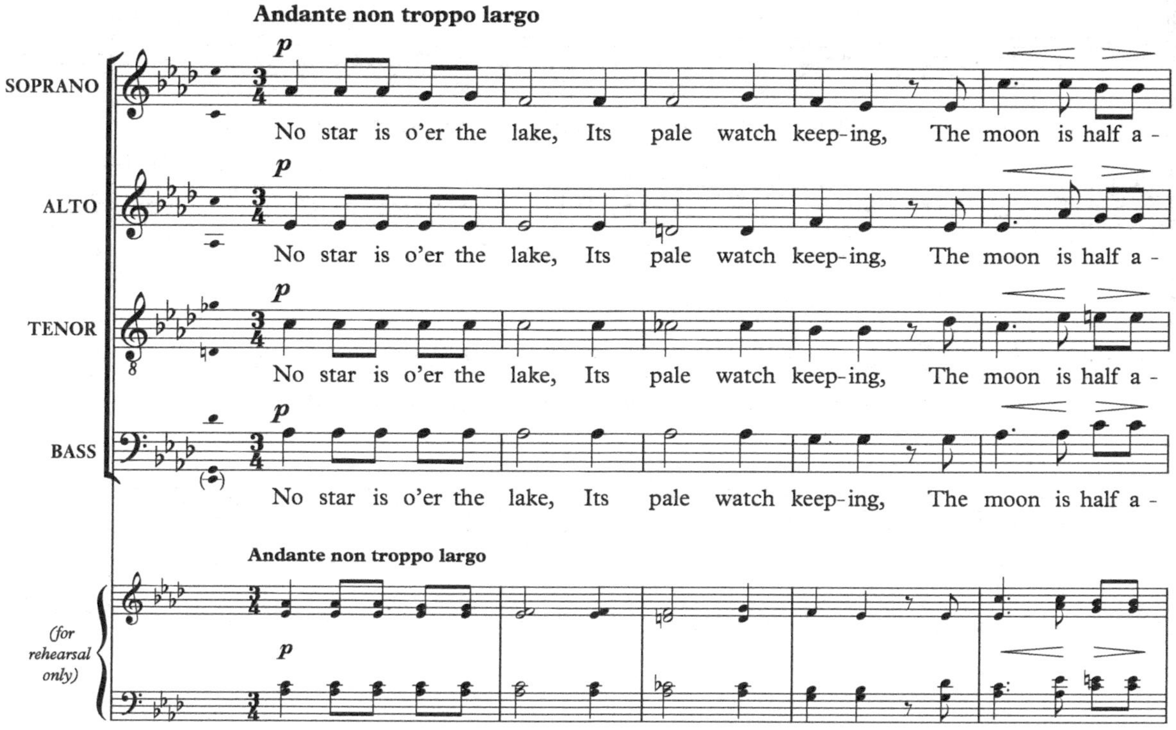

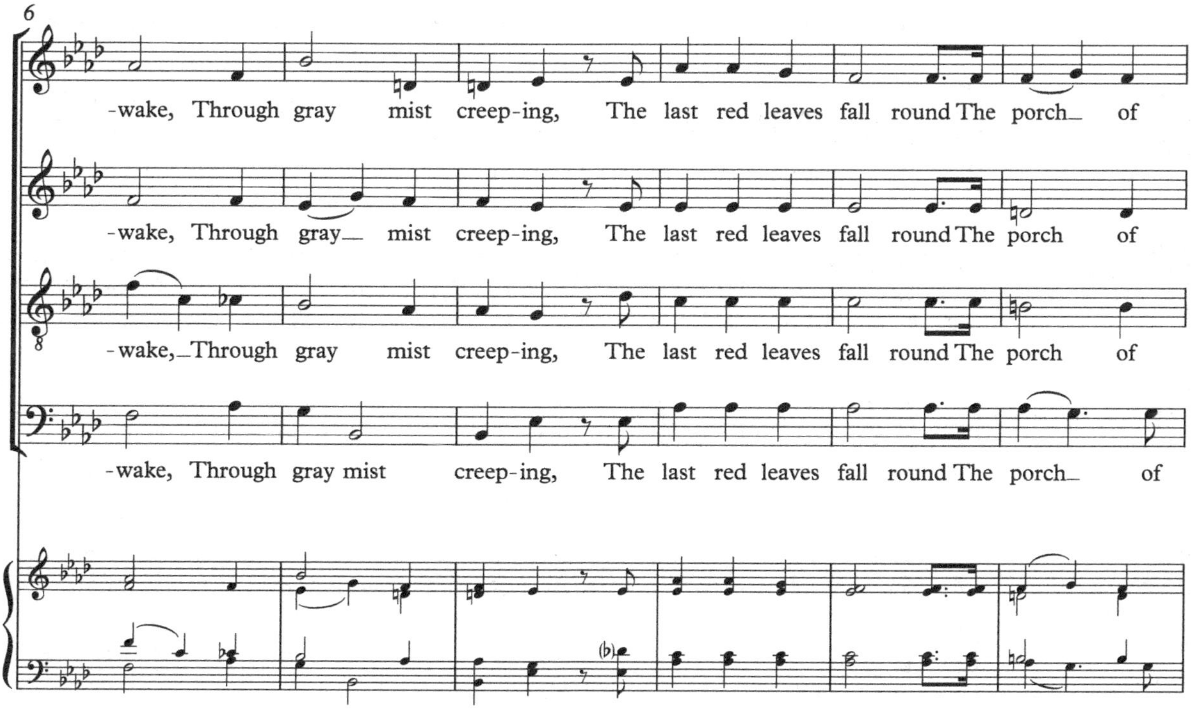

Andante non troppo largo

SOPRANO, ALTO, TENOR, BASS:
No star is o'er the lake, Its pale watch keep-ing, The moon is half a-wake, Through gray mist creep-ing, The last red leaves fall round The porch of

(for rehearsal only)

* The small notes in the bass part are intended for use as additional notes, when the partsong is performed by a chorus.

to Armstrong Gibbs

55. Three Shakespeare Songs

Words by William Shakespeare
(1564–1616)

R. VAUGHAN WILLIAMS
(1872–1958)

1. Full Fathom Five

The Tempest, Act I, Scene 2

* 'Ding', 'dong' and 'bell' should be sung

di - ng
do - ng
be - ll

2. The Cloud-Capp'd Towers

The Tempest, Act IV, Scene 1

3. Over Hill, Over Dale

A Midsummer Night's Dream, Act II, Scene 1

56. Sweet Suffolk owl

Words: Anon.

THOMAS VAUTOR
(*fl.* 1600–20)

57a. Thule, the period of cosmography

The first part

Words: Anon.

THOMAS WEELKES
(1576–1623)

57b. The Andalusian merchant

The second part

58. Draw on, sweet Night

Words: Anon.

JOHN WILBYE
(1574–1638)

* This note may be shortened to a ♩

59. Weep, weep, mine eyes

Words: Anon

JOHN WILBYE
(1574–1638)

(back to p. 361)

COMMENTARY

Notes

1. Specific references to musical notes are given thus: bar number (arabic), stave number counting down from the top stave in each system (roman), symbol number in the bar (arabic). For example, in Bennet's *All creatures now*, 19 ii 1 refers to the length of soprano 2's first note in bar 19.

2. Pitch and rhythmic references are given in terms of this edition, not of the original sources. Where editions are transposed and note values shortened, so are all references to variants unless explicitly described as original.

3. The Helmholtz system of pitch notation has been used whenever it is important to specify the octave of a particular note (except where the octave is self-evident). The seven notes upwards from the C an octave below middle C are shown thus: *c d e f g a b*; the seven notes upwards from middle C are *c' d' e' f' g' a' b'*; the next octave, *c" d"*, etc. The octave two octaves below middle C is *C D*, etc. Notes in roman capitals, C, D, etc., are not octave-specific.

4. Original clefs are indicated by the note they designate (F, C, G) and the line of the stave on which they are placed, starting from the bottom. So G2 is the normal treble clef, C3 is the alto clef and F4 is the bass clef.

1. Anonymous: *Dindirín, dindirín*

The *Cancionero Musical de Palacio* was copied around 1500, perhaps for the court of Ferdinand II, perhaps for the Duke of Alba, at whose castle the main composer included in the MS, Juan del Encina, worked in the 1490s. It contains over 450 pieces, mostly short and secular. This morning song to a nightingale may well use traditional material. It also survives in a manuscript now at Monte Cassino (MS 871) that was copied at a monastery at Gaeta on the Italian coast between Naples and Rome in the late fifteenth century. That version is in three parts, two of which correspond roughly to the alto and bass of the version given here. The words belong to a tradition that goes back to the troubadours in a variety of languages and are in a mixture of Catalan, French, and Italian.

*Source: Madrid, Palacio Real, Biblioteca, II-1335; edited in *Monumentos de la Música Española*, vol. 10, no. 359 (Barcelona, 1951). *Clefs:* C1 C2 C4 F4. *Time signature:* ¢. Note values quartered. *Notes:* Since the text is such a linguistic mix, it is difficult to decide on the pronunciation: a mixture of holiday Spanish and French may not be authentic but will give an appropriate impression of linguistic fluidity. The MS stops at bar 22, giving only the words for the rest of the piece.

2. Arcadelt: *Il bianco e dolce cigno*

The idea that the swan sang as he died was taken by Renaissance poets from two much-read Roman poets, Ovid and Martial. In England it is familiar from Gibbons's *The silver swan* (no. 23), and it is very likely that he knew Arcadelt's setting, since it is the first piece in the most widely circulated madrigal book of the period, with fifty-eight editions appearing between 1538 and 1654. The words are often attributed to Alfonso d'Avalos (1502–1546) on no strong grounds (see no. 47). The attribution to Guidiccioni is not much stronger, resting on the inclusion of the poem in eighteenth-century editions of his poems, though it is not in earlier editions. Arcadelt may have been Flemish or French. He worked in Florence for about a decade, then was appointed to the Sistine Chapel choir in Rome in 1538. From 1552 he worked for the Cardinal of Lorraine and the French court. If the madrigal is sung chorally, altos and tenors might be mixed on the middle two parts.

Source: Il primo libro di madrigali di Archadelt a quatro voci (Venice, 1539); the 1538 edition is not extant.

3. Bartlet: *Of all the birds that I do know*

John Bartlet worked for the Earl of Hertford and became an Oxford Bachelor of Music in 1610. He is known almost solely from his *Booke of Ayres*. Most madrigals and ayres set contemporary poems, but this is from several decades earlier, published in 1573. Philip as a name for a sparrow goes back to the poet Thomas Skelton at the beginning of the century.

Source: A Booke of Ayres (London, 1606). *Clefs:* G2 C2 C3 F4. Black notation (i.e. what looks like a crotchet in the incipit is a coloured minim, so the note values of this edition are halved). Only one verse is underlaid, the rest being printed as verse. No sharp in the original key signature, but all necessary sharps are printed and modernization causes no ambiguities. Lute part omitted. *Notes:* 4 i: the text is printed without any specific indication of whether the second syllable is set to note 2 or note 3. Verse 4, line 5: 'fend cut, Phip' meaning not entirely clear, but perhaps borrowed from fencing meaning something like 'keep the right distance'. (Skelton's *Philip Sparrow* has 'Philip, keep your cut'.) Line 6: 'Peat' is a term of endearment.

4. Bennet: *All creatures now*

The Italian idea of publishing a collection of madrigals in honour of a patron or an event reached England through *Il Trionfi di Dori* of 1592, commissioned by a wealthy Venetian, Leonardo Sanudo, for his bride. Twenty-nine composers each contributed a madrigal, ending with the same congratulatory couplet. *The Triumphes of Oriana* was published in 1601 with no indication of its function; the dedicatory letter (to Charles Howard, Earl of Nottingham) is remarkably uninformative about why Morley assembled or commissioned 'these few discordant tunes', as he modestly called them. All end with the words

Then sang the shepherds and nymphs of Diana
Long live fair Oriana!

The name Oriana is taken from the then-famous romance *Amadis de Gaule*, Oriana being the fair, constant, and chaste beloved of the hero Amadis. In 1601 the name could only refer to Queen Elizabeth I. Many of the texts seem appropriate for singing at ceremonial tournaments, such as those held on the anniversary of the queen's accession or on May Day, but that may be because such events provided appropriate imagery. Oriana is here presiding over a hunting scene, appropriate for Diana, goddess of the chase. The music is illustrative, from the opening laughter to the long notes wishing Oriana a long life. The bugle was at this period an instrument of the hunt, not the battlefield; 'winded' refers to the act of blowing, not of making a curved shape, so should be pronounced accordingly. 'The flowers themselves discover' (that is, the flowers show themselves to view) is perhaps a metaphor from the stage, when the pulling back of the curtain to the inner stage discovers what lies behind.

The original time signature is ¢, not ₵, which is a warning not to hurry: a degree of stateliness should be evident. We have kept to regular barring (the original has no barlines), but have marked triple rhythms in the accompaniment in bars 23–5 and 33–6. Bars 49–55 should be sung as if the barlines were displaced by a minim.

Virtually nothing is known about John Bennet (the name is spelt Benet in the 1601 edition). His *Madrigalls to Foure Voyces* were published in 1599, with a dedication to Ralph Assheton, who held official positions in Chester and Lancashire, offering 'these first fruits of my simple skill'; so he was probably a young man from the north-east.

Source: Madrigales. The Triumphes of Oriana, to 5. and 6. voices: composed by divers severall aucthors. Newly published by Thomas Morley (London, 1601) (*RISM* 160112). Two editions were published in that year. The original price was four shillings and sixpence; at least, that is what the Cavendish family paid in December 1601. *Variants:* 8 v 1: ♩. (no rest) / 9–12: no apostrophe in 'shepherds'; we have assumed more than one of them / 19 ii 1: ♩. (no rest) / 22–3: in all parts 'Orianaes' / 28 iii and iv 3 – 30 iii and iv 1: underlay ambiguous, since only a repetition of the previous phrase is marked; melisma in iv follows the explicitly notated pattern of v in bar 26; ii is also indicated thus, but makes sense with the normal rule of having the melisma on the penultimate syllable / 30 i 1: ♩ ♪ (which is how it should be sung in all parts).

5. Brahms: *Nachtwache No. 1*
Brahms conducted choirs at various stages of his career, including early music and folksong in their repertoire, so it is not surprising that he wrote partsongs. His Op. 104 comprises five pieces, mostly melancholy. This is the first of two to poems by Rückert, from his *Italienische Gedichte*, with the title *Nachtwache*. Brahms set them in 1888, and writers have associated them with the composer's awareness of passing years (though he was only fifty-five).
Source: Fünf Gesänge für gemischten Chor a Cappella (Simrock, Berlin, 1889 [*recte* 1888]); we have omitted

the English translation by Mrs J. P. Morgan printed below the German in that edition; we have also consulted *Johannes Brahms, Sämtliche Werke*, vol. 21. Editorial hairpins have been added to parallel passages.

6. Britten: *The Evening Primrose*
Throughout his life, vocal music was central to Britten's work. One of his most distinctive early works, *A Boy Was Born* (1930), is a set of choral variations of great originality. In his operas, the emphasis is chiefly on the solo voice (though there is magnificent choral writing in *Peter Grimes*), but he returned to the vocal ensemble in his last illness for *Sacred and Profane*. He had a fine taste in poetry—not surprising for a close friend of W. H. Auden—and his *Five Flower Songs* of 1950 sets poems by Herrick, Crabbe, Clare, and Anon. John Clare spent the first half of his life in Helpston, a small village in Northamptonshire; he had considerable success with his first book of poems in 1820, but returned to rural life (he had worked as a gardener and farm labourer) and spent much of the rest of his life in asylums. Britten's songs were written for the twenty-fifth wedding anniversary of Leonard and Dorothy Elmhirst, who had bought the run-down Dartington estate in Devon in the 1920s and had restored it to be a place of beauty and the home of a progressive school; the music summer school came later (1953). They were generous patrons of Britten's English Opera Group.
Source: Five Flower Songs for mixed chorus (Boosey and Hawkes, London, [1951]). *Notes:* in earlier music in this book, unaccented quavers beginning a bar (as in bars 1 and 3) would be treated as if upbeats; but performers will need to decide whether the barline and the first syllable of the poetic line encourages slightly more weight / bars 5–6 show another typical feature of earlier styles: the use of three-note phrases crossing the metrical pattern.

7. Campion: *Never weather-beaten sail*
Thomas Campion (or Campian) came from a wealthier background than most of the musicians of his time. He was well educated, having studied at Cambridge and at Grays Inn, perhaps chiefly for social reasons, and also obtained a medical degree at Caen in Normandy. He wrote poetry in Latin and English as well as books on poetry and counterpoint, and he was involved in the production of court masques. He published four books of songs to his own words, distinguished by a simplicity of style in which words and music matched perfectly. This comes from the first book, which was intended for domestic use.
Source: Two Bookes of Ayres. The First Contayning Divine and Morall Songs . . . (London, *c.*1613). Lute part omitted. The edition has only verse 1 underlaid, but prints both verses separately, Campion presumably wishing to set out his texts as poetry. The underlay is too squashed to indicate precise placement of syllables beneath quavers; in bar 10, for instance, the third syllable of the alto part could be sung a note earlier. The inconsistency between the parts of the original time signatures is by no means rare, and suggests that they were not of great significance (cf. no. 11). The original

edition indicates bars 5–8 by a repeat of bars 1–4 and marks bars 9–18 to be repeated, though the presence of double bars after bar 12 is unusual and makes one wonder whether only bars 13–18 should be repeated; the repeat pattern AABCC, with different text for the repeat of A but not of C, is quite common: see, for example, Ford's *Since first I saw your face* (no. 19). Repetition in music comprising short sections was normal at this period, whether signs were present or not. When present, they can be ambiguous: ‖: need not imply a repeat of both the preceding and following sections since :‖ and ‖: are never used. One possibility is to sing verse 1 with no repeats, but to repeat 13–18 in verse 2. *Variants:* 9 iii 7: ♯ omitted, but confirmed by the lute part / 11 ii 2: *e'*, changed to *g'* in accordance with the lute part.

8. Cornelius: *So weich und warm*
Cornelius's parents were actors and he was prepared for a career as actor and musician. He became a poet and music critic and spent five years (1853–8) in Weimar working for Liszt, who encouraged him as a composer. He then moved to Vienna and Munich, where he was an associate of Wagner. His literary skills enabled him to write the libretti for his operas and also the texts for many of his songs. In a period which favoured orchestral music, he wrote surprisingly little music without words. He is known in the English-speaking world for just one work, *The Three Kings*, a song whose piano accompaniment (based on a chorale) was arranged for choir by Ivor Atkins in 1930. *So weich und warm* was written as an unaccompanied duet for soprano and alto around 1848, when Cornelius was living with his uncle, the painter Peter von Cornelius, in Berlin. The four-voice arrangement given here, with an extended text, was his last composition, probably finished by his pupil Karl Hoffbauer. In bars 19–20, 'mutterseelenallein' literally means 'alone without your mother's soul'.
Source: Musikalische Werke Band II (Breitkopf & Härtel, Leipzig, 1905).

9. Debussy: *Trois chansons de Charles d'Orléans*
The prince-poet Charles d'Orléans, nephew of one French king and father of another, wrote much of his poetry—some in French, some in English—during a twenty-five-year period of imprisonment in England after being taken hostage at the Battle of Agincourt in 1415. His captivity seems not to have been without pleasant diversions: the dedicatee of some of his love poetry (including *Dieu! qu'il la fait bon regarder*) is reputed to have been Alice Chaucer, descendant of the famous poet and wife of the Duke of Suffolk, his guardian at Wingfield Manor, where he was kept for a time.
Debussy was attracted by Charles d'Orléans's poetry. In a letter of 1908 to his friend Louis Laloy requesting clarification of the meaning of some archaic words in *Quant j'ay ouy le tabourin*, he wrote: 'I find this little poem so full of sweet interior music that—naturally—I cannot stop myself from "exteriorizing" it . . .'. His setting of this whimsical *rondel* was the last of the three chansons to be composed: nos. 1 and 3 were written ten years earlier in 1898, for a small amateur choir in Passy

which Debussy directed at that time, the nucleus of which was provided by the family of his friend Lucien Fontaine (whose singing Debussy likened to 'un taureau sentimental'). From the absence of *divisis* in these two settings, it is possible that the 'choir' may not have been much more than a quartet.
The two chansons remained unpublished until 1908, when no. 2 was added and no. 3 substantially rewritten; the set of three was then premièred at the Concerts Colonne in Paris in 1909, with the composer conducting. All three were enthusiastically received by the audience, nos. 2 and 3 being encored, and a slightly revised version of the set was published in 1910.
The *Trois chansons* are most attractively varied in style and mood. No. 1, despite its archaically modal flattened seventh, is closest to the harmonically seductive Debussy of the *Prélude à l'après-midi d'un faune*. No. 2, more austere, uses the altos, tenors, and basses instrumentally to evoke the drums of a May Day procession, underpinning the languid solo of the young man who prefers to stay home in solitude rather than join in the fun. *Yver, vous n'estes qu'un villain*, which is loosely inspired by Renaissance choral style, neatly contrasts grim winter and pleasant summer by characterizing minor-key winter with contrapuntal imitation (a device viewed with distaste by Debussy) and major-key summer with sweet homophony.
The distinctive and deliberately historical French quality of the *Trois chansons de Charles d'Orléans* undoubtedly provided Ravel with the model for his own delightful *Trois chansons* of 1915, and we can only regret that neither composer left any further works for *a cappella* choir, a medium for which they both wrote so effectively. *Source:* revised published edition (Durand, Paris, 1910); also consulted: composer's MS (Paris, Bibliothèque Nationale, MS 192). There are only minor discrepancies between the MS and published versions, with the important exception of the voice assigned to the solo in no. 2. In the MS this is tenor (its part written in the treble clef on a stave between the alto and choral tenor staves), but a later correction in the composer's hand crossed out 'Ténor solo' and substituted 'Contralto solo', adding a note to the engraver, 'le Contralto solo au dessus', a change followed in the published edition. Why did Debussy make this change? The character in the poem is surely male, and from a musical standpoint the part is perfectly effective for tenor, though admittedly slightly low-lying. Neither a female alto nor a male countertenor seems to the present editor quite right, and conductors may prefer to follow Debussy's first thought and use a tenor. *Note:* exceptionally in this volume, the original beaming of notes has been preserved; the presence of Debussy's own phrase slurs makes the addition of editorial syllabic slurs undesirable, and in the absence of the latter the verbal underlay is perhaps clearer if separate tails are used for notes carrying a separate syllable. Spelling, punctuation, and capitalization of the text follow the 1910 edition. [J.R.]

10. Delius: *To be sung of a summer night on the water*
Frederick Delius's father was a successful businessman, working in the wool trade, who had moved to Bradford

368

from Bielefeld and had become a British citizen before Frederick was born. His family was musical, but did not approve of a career for him in that profession. Attempts to develop Delius's interest in the wool trade were unsuccessful, and a period working at a Florida orange plantation was valuable chiefly for his opportunity to hear black singers. Most of his music required a large orchestra, and the characteristic lushness of sound is carried over into these two wordless choruses, written in 1917. The opening bars of the second piece quote two ubiquitous nursery songs of the time: the opening of 'Have you seen the muffin man (who lives down Drury Lane)' and 'Madam will you walk, Madam will you talk (Madam will you walk and talk with me)?', the refrain of 'I will give you the keys of heaven'. (I quote the titles as I remember them; some informants favour 'Do you know the muffin man?'.)

'These two delightful pieces have long been favourites among choir directors, but are not performed as often as they deserve because the awkwardness of their part-writing makes them needlessly difficult for singers. Delius devised his exquisite chains of chromatic harmony without much regard for the detail of individual voice parts. The present edition preserves virtually all the notes of the originals, but with some interchanging and adjustment of voice parts to make the individual lines more singable. Both pieces may effectively be sung a semitone lower.' [J.R.]

Sources: original version, Winthrop Rogers, London, 1920, dedicated 'For Kennedy Scott and the Oriana Choir' (they gave the first performance on 28 June 1921); John Rutter edition, Oxford University Press, 1991.

11. Dowland: *Come, heavy sleep*
Dowland was a lutenist with an international reputation. In the 1590s he travelled in Germany and Italy and was suspected of treason because of his Catholic contacts. He worked as lutenist to the King of Denmark from 1598 to 1606, then returned to London, though did not receive the court appointment he felt was his due. He published his *First Booke of Songes or Ayres* in 1597; it was an enormous success and set the pattern for such publications.

Source: The First Booke of Songes or Ayres of fowre partes with Tablature for the Lute (London, 1597). Lute part omitted. The awkwardness of underlay of verse 2 can be diminished in 5 i and 18 iv by ignoring the rests and by making a slight crescendo through bar 4. *Variants:* 8 ii 2: ♯, but ♮ in lute part / 24: text 'thoughts worn' in all parts. We have preserved the normal modern amendment, which agrees, apart from the modern hyphen, with the version of the poem set by Robert Johnson (printed in original spelling in Diana Poulton, *John Dowland* (London, 1972, p. 243), chiefly because it is easier to sing. The changes in later editions (which mostly concern the lute part) are not noted here except the correction of 'his' (stanza 2, bars 11–12) to 'this'.

12. Dowland: *Can she excuse my wrongs*
Source: The First Booke of Songes or Ayres of fowre partes with Tablature for the Lute (London, 1597). Lute part omitted. The music also exists as an instrumental

piece with the title *The Earl of Essex's Galliard* and makes a perfectly good piece without the words (as in Dowland's *Lachrimae*, for five strings and lute, of 1604). The poem may have been written by or on behalf of the queen's impetuous favourite, the Earl of Essex, whose rise and fall is told in Britten's opera *Gloriana*. For bars 33–6, the rhythm changes to 6/8 and the middle parts allude in canon to a popular song, *The woods so wild*. Bars 9–16 and 25–31 are printed once with double underlay in the original. *Variants:* 2 i 2: this note is flattened in some of the many instrumental versions of the tune and also in the accompaniment in the first three editions, though the later editions avoid the B. The original edition has no key signature (the natural in this edition is the consequence of modernizing the signature), and it is possible that a singer of the time would have expected the note to have been flattened without the need for an accidental, especially as the tune may well already have been familiar (there are sources of it dated a year or two before the first edition); but other versions of the melody in tablature (which are not dependent on key signatures) have a natural. The tune seems to have circulated in both forms. / 4 iv: ♩ ♪ / 24 ii: no dot / 38 iii 2: superfluous sharp.

13. Dowland: *Weep you no more, sad fountains*
Many lute songs are essentially homophonic and can equally well be performed as lute solos or in four parts, but the fluidity of the part-writing and the gratefulness of the words for singing make performance of this song by a vocal ensemble preferable. Although we have not added dynamics, it is obvious that each verse has a long diminuendo from the soprano g" in bar 18; the temptation to slow down is more easily resisted if the bass is treated as a melodic line leading to the penultimate bar, not just the harmonic basis.

Source: The Third and Last Booke of Songs or Aires (London, 1603). Lute part omitted. *Variants:* 4 iv 3: e♭ in the bass is added to correspond with original signature / 6 iv 2: e♮ is editorial, confirmed by lute part / 27: Dowland's lute part has a bottom D, which low basses may sing.

14. Elgar: *As torrents in summer*
Elgar was born near Worcester, the son of a piano tuner. He spent much of his life in the area, and was particularly attached to the Malvern Hills. His career began as a jobbing freelance violinist. He composed an enormous amount, at first with only local success, but his ambition was encouraged by the determination of his wife (he married above his station in 1889). He achieved some popularity during the 1890s with a series of secular cantatas, then suddenly achieved success with the *Enigma Variations* in 1899. *As torrents in summer* is an independent partsong in *Scenes from the Saga of King Olaf*, Op. 30, written for the North Staffordshire Musical Festival, October 1896. Longfellow's poem was adapted by a neighbour of the Elgars, Harry Acworth. The story is complicated: a genealogical table showing how the characters in it are related has nearly forty names. Fortunately, this metaphorical chorus from Olaf's death scene needs no context to justify it, and

indeed Elgar was anticipating that it might be published separately while he was correcting the proofs of the vocal score in May 1896.
Source: Scenes from the Saga of King Olaf, Op. 30 (Novello, London, 1896), pp. 163–5; separate edition as Novello's Part-Song Book (Second Series), PSB no. 796. *Variants: Andantino* in PSB only / 5: both editions have *ten.* marked for staves i and ii, with stress marks staff i only; bars 6, 25, and 26 should presumably be sung similarly / 6 iii 1–2: the piano accompaniment (which is Elgar's own) implies that these two notes be sung as ♩♪ / 43: ♩ in *King Olaf*, with orchestral continuation starting at the beginning of the bar.

15. Elgar: *My love dwelt in a Northern land*

This is among Elgar's earliest partsongs, written in 1890 to a poem by Andrew Lang published in the *Century Magazine* in May 1882. It was the first work of Elgar to be published by the leading English publisher of choral music, Novello. Elgar got 100 free copies but no fee, and had to pay the poet a guinea for his permission, which was granted reluctantly on the third request. Elgar wrote of it to his friend Jaeger ('Nimrod') in 1908, 'Now a stock piece for superior poetic choirs: then [1890] it was said to be crude, ill-written for the voices, laid out without knowledge of the capabilities of the human voice &c&c!!'.
Source: My love dwelt in a Northern land, Novello's Part-Song Book (Second Series), PSB no. 585. Publication of Op. 18 as a set did not occur until 1979.

16. Elgar: *There is sweet music*

The set of four partsongs written in Rome at the end of 1907 and early 1908 shows Elgar at his most ambitious in this form, and it was tempting to include the whole set. This is the first of the set and is the least-often sung, chiefly because it looks so difficult; but despite the separate key signatures for each choir, the difficulty is primarily for the rehearsal pianist. Elgar wrote 'No. 1 is, of course, written as it is for *convenience*', so we have had no compunction in renotating the piano part in a way that seems to us to be less complicated. In the same letter (26 April 1908), he writes that 'short syllables may be sustained occasionally for the sake of effect', and stresses that, 'a modern partsong is to be listened to and not read'. The words are from Tennyson's *The Lotos-Eaters*. It was dedicated to Canon Gorton, Rector of Morecambe, who organized a local competitive choral festival; Elgar had visited him in Morecambe in 1903 and had conducted a specially written partsong to an audience of 6000.
Source: Four Part-Songs, Op. 53 No. 1 (Novello, London, 1908), Novello's Part-Song Book (Second Series), PSB no. 1056.

17. Farmer: *Fair Phyllis I saw sitting all alone*

Farmer is first heard of in 1591, when he published a collection of canons while still 'in youth'. Like his single book of madrigals, it was dedicated to the Earl of Oxford, so he may have been supported by him. He spent part of the 1590s as organist at Christ Church Cathedral, Dublin, but was back in London when his madrigal book was published. This is one of the lightest madrigals. It is difficult to sing 'whither she was gone' without overemphasizing the consonants: it helps to accent the first note of each group of four quavers and lighten the rest. We have preserved from the original notation the soprano part's retention of duple time in bars 32–3 and 52–3 while the lower parts sing in 6/4 (original time signature 𝄴 in black notation): the tempo relationship is unambiguous.
Source: The First Set of English Madrigals (London, 1599). Bars 1–7: repeat printed out in full. *Variant:* 6: i and ii, 'mountain side'; iii and iv, 'mountains side'.

18. Finzi: *My spirit sang all day*

Finzi's music was highly regarded during his lifetime, though not particularly popular. His outstanding work is the song-cycle *Dies natalis*, to mystical poems by Thomas Traherne. Choral singers know him for his set of seven partsongs to words by Robert Bridges, a poet whose reputation was in decline before the end of his long life and which has not revived. This is the third item of that set.
Source: My spirit sang all day (Oxford University Press, London, 1937).

19. Ford: *Since first I saw your face*

Ford worked at the English court from 1611 until 1642. His single publication is the only indication of his earlier career. This contains eleven songs and eighteen pieces for viol. The two best-known songs, this and *There is a lady sweet and kind*, are the most straightforward in the collection; Ford's music is elsewhere more elaborate if less charming.
Source: Musicke of Sundrie Kindes (London, 1607). Lute part omitted. *Variants:* 3 ii 4 and 7 ii 4: *g'* (though one wonders whether Ford was very concerned about consecutives) / 13 i 1: rest omitted / 14 and 15: comma after 'fast' in tenor part only / 14 iii 3–4: ♩♩ ; the lute part, doubling the alto line but not the tenor, has ♪♪ / 15–16: two four-beat bars and a concluding two-beat bar / 15–16 lute: omits the soprano part as normal; instead 𝄞♩♪♩♪♩♪𝄂 thus filling the open third on the last chord.

20. Gabrieli: *Lieto godea*

Giovanni Gabrieli's name is synonymous with polychoral music (music set out for more than one choir), although he did not invent the style and his understanding of the word 'choir' was rather different from ours. He may just as well have intended *Lieto godea*, which is described in the 1587 edition as being 'per cantar et sonar', to have been performed by two voices and six instruments as by two four-voice choirs. His pupil Schütz incorporated it as an instrumental interlude in his setting of Psalm 111 (SWV 34), and other composers also based compositions on it. Gabrieli probably studied with his uncle Andrea and, like him, worked for a while with Lassus at Munich. Thereafter, he remained in his native Venice, being one of the two organists at the Basilica of San Marco and also acting as an entrepreneur. There is a report by an English tourist, Thomas Coryat, of a concert for the patronal festival at the Scuola di San Rocco (performed amid the Tintorettos) which can be matched with the surviving list of fees paid to the musicians: Gabrieli received a substantial 'present', presumably for composing and/or organizing, and also a fee for hiring the seven organs which Coryat mentions. Conductors need to decide how to handle the echoes: making the second statement of each pair quieter is only one of the possible options. If the two choirs are sufficiently separate, or are differently constituted, there may be no need to make any further dynamic contrast. In the one work in which Gabrieli included dynamic marks, the instrumental *Sonata pian' e forte* (1597), the sections where each choir plays separately are marked *piano* and those where they play together *forte*.

Source: Concerti di Andrea et di Gio. Gabrieli (Venice, 1587), (*RISM* 1587[12]). *Clefs:* G2, C1, C3, F3 each choir. These clefs imply downward transposition of a fourth or fifth: we have taken it down only a major third. Instrumental parts for a flexible scoring with modern instruments are available from the publisher; other transpositions and instrumental parts notated at sounding pitch and suitable for modern or early instruments are published by King's Music. *Time signature:* ¢; bar 25 ¢3.

21. Gastoldi: *Amor vittorioso*

Gastoldi worked as a church musician in Mantua. His church compositions, however, were outshone by his set of vocal *balletti*, a form which he virtually invented. The alternation of light texts with 'fa la la's proved particularly popular in England and Germany, and they were translated as well as imitated (often very closely) by Morley and Hassler (see nos. 41 and 25). The military metaphor of the poem comes through clearly in the music, and a marching tempo should be adopted, though it is often sung more quickly. A military precision should not, however, prevent de-accenting the second minim in bars 2, 4, etc. If you have a chance, try dancing it.

Source: Balletti . . . con li suoi Versi per cantare, sonare, & ballare (Venice, 1591).

22. Gibbons: *Ah, dear heart*

Orlando's father was a wait (a town musician) at Cambridge and Oxford, and his son Christopher became one of the leading musicians in the mid-seventeenth century. Orlando was a choirboy at King's College, Cambridge, and became organist at the Chapel Royal in 1605. Orlando died suddenly at Canterbury on 5 June 1625, the Chapel Royal having gone there to receive Charles I's bride, Henrietta Maria. Doctors reported 'In the braine wee founde the whole & sole cause of his sicknes namely a great admirable blackness & syderation in the outside of the braine'. Although not a pupil of Byrd, of all his generation Gibbons was the composer most influenced by him. His madrigals are far less Italianate than those of his contemporaries, and often are effective as solos with instrumental accompaniment. The words of 'Ah, dear heart' are almost the same as those of a song by Dowland printed in *A Pilgrim's Solace* (1612) which begins 'Stay, O

sweet, and do not rise'. With yet another opening, 'Lie still my dear', it is attributed to John Donne in a 1669 edition of his poems, but modern scholars reject the attribution. Dowland prints a second stanza, but it does not fit Gibbons's setting.

Source: The First Set of Madrigals and Mottets of 5. Parts: apt for Viols and Voyces (London, 1612). *Notes:* the range of the original tenor part is awkward; we have allocated it to alto for bars 1–25 and interchanged the parts for bars 26–35. In places like bars 16 (soprano and bass) and 26, the opening crotchet should be treated as an upbeat with the accent on the minim.

23. Gibbons: *The silver swan*

Unlike most of the sixteenth- and seventeenth-century pieces here, this has been in the vocal repertoire ever since it was written and has not needed modern revival. For the dying swan myth, see Arcadelt's *Il bianco e dolce cigno* (no. 2).

Source: The First Set of Madrigals and Mottets of 5. Parts: apt for Viols and Voyces (London, 1612).

24. Gibbons: *What is our life?*

The ascription of this fine poem to Sir Walter Raleigh comes from some poetic manuscripts of the period, though the comment in one that it was written 'the same morning he was executed' must have been surmised by a scribe who did not know that Gibbons had published his setting six years earlier. Its sombre, sustained style justifies the use of the word motet in the title of the volume. Gibbons is inconsistent whether 'passion' has two or three syllables. This is particularly clear in the first tenor part, where at its first occurrence there are only two notes, immediately followed by a repeat in which it is given three notes and is printed with hyphens dividing it into three syllables. 'Di-vi-si-on', with which it rhymes, is printed thus in that part, but as 'di-vi-sion' in the other parts; it is, however, always set to music that implies a four-syllable division. 'Division' is the term for a form of embellishment in which long notes are split (divided) into roulades or shorter ones, hence the quavers to which it is set. The speed needs to be fast enough to maintain the unity of the long phrases. Make the most of the way Gibbons disrupts the regular rhythm at 'Thus march we playing', treating 'march' as a downbeat wherever it occurs.

Source: The First Set of Madrigals and Mottets of 5. Parts: apt for Viols and Voyces (London, 1612).

25. Hassler: *Tanzen und springen (Gagliarda)*

Hassler was the son of an amateur organist at Nuremberg. In 1584–5 he studied in Venice with Andrea Gabrieli, the first of many Germans who would travel there for instruction, and also became a friend of Andrea's nephew Giovanni, whose *Lieto godea* (no. 20) he imitated. He worked for the wealthy Fugger family in Augsburg until 1600. He then spent four years back in Nuremberg as the town's director of music, another four at Ulm, and his final four years at the court of Christian II of Saxony at Dresden. Although now less well known than Michael Praetorius, he was the leading German composer of his time. *Tantzen und springen* (the underlaid text is modernized, but the original spelling is a reminder that in German the 'z' includes an initial 't' sound) is an imitation of Gastoldi's *balletti* (see no. 21). *Source: Lustgarten* (Nuremberg, 1601). Only the first verse is underlaid.

26. Hassler: *Ach, Weh des Leiden*

This is printed next to *Tanzen und springen* in *Lustgarten* but it is very different. The feature of the triple-time section that distinguishes it from a dance is the balancing of a two-bar phrase by one in three bars. In the duple time section, 'Muss ich dich dann aufgeben' is set with a different rhythm in each part, preparing for genuine counterpoint (the upper two parts in canon) from 'So kost's mir'. Triple time at this period is not normally slow or heavy, so the initial grief should not be laid on too thickly.
Source: Lustgarten (Nuremberg, 1601). *Variants:* 20: time signature ₵ / 34–end: none of the Es are flattened in the original edition. The explicit E♭s in the soprano parts in bars 31 and 32 would have given a strong hint to singers to continue to flatten Es, but performers may like to experiment with E♮s.

27. Haydn: *Die Harmonie in der Ehe (Matrimonial harmony)*

Haydn wrote one of the most popular works for chorus and orchestra in the repertoire, *The Creation*, but his music for smaller vocal ensembles is far less known. During his London visits he had heard far more of such music than he could have done in Vienna and on his return there began setting poems selected from an anthology entitled *Lyrische Blumenlese*, assembled by C. W. Ramler (1725–98), which deliberately withheld the names of their authors so that the reader would judge them on merit, not the fame of the poet. Haydn intended to set twenty-four of them, but only produced thirteen, mostly during 1796. The traditional way to deal with the inconclusive end is to whisper the last phrase, though other solutions are possible.
Source: autograph manuscript, Paris, Bibliothèque Nationale, Conservatoire MS 140, as edited in Joseph Haydn, *Werke*, vol. 30 (Henle Verlag, Munich, 1958). The autograph has a figured bass as the accompaniment, although later items in the collection (nos. 10–13) have a two-stave keyboard. The figuring is very full and includes both parts in the duet sections. But the accompaniment has no independent material, so may be omitted. This edition prints the piano part added (probably not by Haydn) in the first edition (in the *Oeuvres de J. Haydn*, cahier 8, no. 7, Breitkopf & Härtel, Leipzig, 1803). The dynamics also come from that edition, and were probably added by the publisher. *Notes:* bar 6, 'lombert', from the Spanish card game *el hombre*, the 'hombre' being the man who attempts to win the stakes. The 1803 edition has different words from the end of bar 4 to bar 8, perhaps because the original was too obscure: 'Er zechet gern, sie auch; er spielet gern, sie auch; er zählt Dukaten gern'. *Variants:* 41 iii 3–4: *c'*, corrected to fit Haydn's figuring and the piano accompaniment / 52 and 53: grace notes in the voice parts changed from quavers to semiquavers to show performance length (confirmed by the 1803 piano accompaniment).

28. Isaac: *Innsbruck, ich muss dich lassen*

Isaac called himself 'de Flandria', but nothing is known about him until 1484, when he was paid as a composer at Innsbruck. He worked at Florence from the following year and retained connections there after his appointment in 1497 as composer to the emperor, Maximilian I, based in Vienna but travelling elsewhere within Austria. Isaac returned to Florence in 1515, where he died. He was among the most distinguished composers of his time, with an international reputation, but is remembered chiefly for this single brief song. It circulated as a hymn with the title *O Welt, ich muss dich lassen* from the sixteenth century and the tune then became associated with Paul Gerhardt's *Nun ruhen alle Wälder*. Non-Germans know it from its use in Bach's *St Matthew Passion*. In view of the lateness of the sources, the attribution to Isaac may be questioned; and it is likely that the tune and words existed before the setting was made, so biographical speculation is unnecessary. The canonic setting printed here for verse 2 is the second 'Christe eleison' of Isaac's *Missa carminum*, which is based on well-known songs of the period; this movement circulated independently with the German words.
Source: Ein Aussug guter alter und newer teutscher Liedlein (Nuremberg, 1539) (*RISM* 1539[27]). *Variants:* 28 i 3: ♮ in the posthumous edition of the mass (*RISM* 1541[1]); if that is adopted, 29 iv 1 should also be ♮; 28 iii 2 may stay sharp, but should be changed to ♩♪.

29. Jones: *Farewell, dear love*

Despite graduating as a Bachelor of Music at Oxford in 1597, Jones seems to be the least competent of the composers who published madrigals and songs, though as this piece shows, he can write a good tune (if it is his). The original publication has only the first verse underlaid, and the subsequent verses do not always fit very well; a soloist singing to the lute might well adapt them to the notes rather more freely. The words are quoted in Shakespeare's *Twelfth Night*, Act II, scene iii, sung in a rowdy manner by Sir Toby and the clown. The song circulated widely (perhaps it existed before Jones set it, though his version is the earliest one that survives). Jones set a reply, *Farewell, fond youth*, in his *Musicall Dreame* (1609).
Source: The First Booke of Songes and Ayres of Foure Parts (London, 1600). Lute part omitted. *Variant:* verse 1, 9 i 1: 'Nay'; 'Yet' in other parts. *Note:* bar 16: 'moe' means 'more'.

30. Josquin Des Prez: *Mille regrets*

Despite being the major composer of the decades around 1500, surprisingly little is known about Josquin, and that has diminished rather than increased as a result of recent research: much of what seemed to be known about his earlier life turns out to have been the result of confusion with a different Josquin. He worked in Milan in the 1480s, in the papal chapel from 1489 to the mid 1490s, then in France for a while, before a brief spell in

Ferrara in 1503–4. He spent his remaining years at Condé-sur-l'Escaut, now on the Franco-Belgian border. A large amount of music ascribed to him has survived, but scholars are questioning the authenticity of a considerable proportion of it, including this poignant chanson. It was first printed in an anthology, *Chansons musicales a quatre parties*, published in Paris in 1533, where it is ascribed to J. Lemaire; this may be a matter of confusing poet and composer, since Lemaire is not otherwise known as a composer. The earliest attribution to Josquin is at the heading to a vihuela transcription by Luis de Narváez published in 1538, which is headed 'La cancion del Emperador del quarto tono de Jusquin'. Whoever wrote it, it is an expressive though frustratingly short piece; it can be extended in a concert by having a lutenist or guitarist play Narváez's transcription (published in *Monumentos de la Música Española*, vol. 3). The Spanish composer Morales used the chanson as the basis for a mass for six voices (vol. 11 in the same series) and Gombert reworked the chanson for six voices.

Source: L'unziesme livre contenant vingt et neuf chansons amoureuses (Antwerp, 1549) (*RISM* 1549²⁹), where it is followed by a response by the publisher, Tielman Susato: *Les miens aussi brief.* Some regard has been paid to the Narváez version and to other lute transcriptions, especially with respect to the accidentals: the 1549 anthology has none in this piece, and very few in any others either; singers were supposed to know when to add them.

31. Lassus: *Chi chi li chi*

Lassus was the most comprehensive master of music in the second half of the sixteenth century. His output was extraordinary in both quantity and quality. The bulk of his work is set to Latin texts (60 masses, 100 magnificats, 500 motets—not all to religious texts), but he also produced a large number of settings of secular Italian, French, and German texts. He was born at Mons, travelled to Italy as a boy, worked in Rome in 1553, was in Antwerp in 1555, then from 1556 until his death worked for Duke Albrecht V of Bavaria and his successor, Wilhelm V, in Munich. In 1568, Lassus was responsible for the lavish music celebrating the wedding of Wilhelm to Princess Renée of Lorraine. A full account of the event was published, giving very full details of the music and how it was performed. This included performances of *moresche* by six flutes and six voices. Like most of the other *villanesche* and *moresche*, *Chi chi li chi* is based on a Neapolitan piece in popular style, a *morescha* by Giovanni Domino da Nola, perhaps originally sung at a carnival or some other occasion when the normal decencies were relaxed, and accompanied by lewd gestures. The gender confusion of the text may also have comic possibilities: both Martin and the cock are grammatically feminine. It is not at all clear how the dialogue is divided between the characters beyond the opening four bars. Lassus had a reputation as a skilled mime in *commedia dell'arte*; one can imagine the music accompanying a mimed representation of the dialogue. It should be sung with a suitable vigour, dramatic flexibility, and awareness of the rhythm. Note, for instance, that after the first two notes, the opening tutti phrase should sound as if it is in 3/4. (It is not notated thus, since Lassus uses the change to triple time at bar 12 to indicate a faster triple time.) Most performances treat 'Sona se voi sonare' at bar 76 as words to speak (or usually shout), but it may mean repeat bars 71–6 sounding like an instrument. The chords are more characteristic of a lute or cittern than the bagpipe mentioned in the text; perhaps bars 71–2 could be sung several times before going on to bars 73–6, with the top parts (or two solo singers in a choral performance) inventing elaborate runs above the chords.

Source: Libro de villanelle moresche, et altre canzoni (Paris, 1581). We have not attempted to modernize the text, which is probably intended to suggest how a black African whose native language is Arabic might speak a Neapolitan dialect. In a few places, erratic underlay in one part has been corrected to conform with the others.

32. Lassus: *La nuit froide et sombre*

Lassus had a close relationship with the French court. In 1571 he was given control over the publication of his own music in France by Charles IV, who three years later granted him a generous state pension. The official court printers Le Roy and Ballard issued a substantial collection of his music in 1570, revising and expanding it in 1576 to contain 129 pieces, mostly settings of French texts; the title page claims that it was *revuez* (revised or perhaps just approved) by the composer. Du Bellay was a friend of Ronsard and one of the leading poets of his time. The low compass of the opening suits the music so well that we have not transposed it, despite the low range of the alto part. It can be sung a tone or a minor third higher, or the voices can be redistributed with sopranos and altos taking the soprano part, tenors the alto part and baritones the tenor part. The way the music illustrates the words so closely shows Lassus bringing the style of the Italian madrigal into the French chanson, which tended to be more concerned with structure and poise than text expression.

Source: Les meslanges d'Orlande de Lassus (Paris, 1576).

33. Lassus: *Bonjour mon cœur*

Ronsard's poem was published in *La nouvelle continuation des amours* (Paris, 1556); Lassus set only the first of its two verses. Shape the rhythm by following the word stresses, but remember that French accents are less bold than Italian.

Source: Les meslanges d'Orlande de Lassus (Paris, 1576). *Variant:* 12: Lassus set 'tourterelle', but that anticipates bar 24, so Ronsard's original text has been substituted.

34. Lassus: *Matona, mia cara*

This is sometimes performed with an inappropriate beauty by singers who have not understood what it is about. It is in bad Italian, sung by a German soldier promising a woman a full night's activity. The problem is to balance the suavity of the music with the situation it dramatizes. The translation is far more innocent than the original text, especially 'cazze' and 'ficar'.

Source: Libro de villanelle, moresche, et altre canzoni (Paris, 1581).

35. Le Jeune: *Revoici venir du printemps*

Claude Le Jeune was a native of Valencienne and is first known from four chansons published in 1554. He was the leading composer linked to a group of poets, led by Baïf, who established the Académie de Poésie et de Musique for the cultivation of *musique mesurée à l'antique*. This involved the creation of poems following the metres of Latin poets such as Horace and setting them in chordal declamation according to the rhythmic pattern of long and short notes demanded by Latin prosody. Most of his music was collected together in a series of publications after his death. *Le printemps* includes a brief 'Preface sur la musique mesurée' praising the composer for restoring the rhythmic parameter of music to its place alongside harmony.
Source: Le printemps (Paris, 1603) and *Airs* (Paris, 1608). *Note:* the texts of the 1608 edition were revised to make the verse rhyme; this edition preserves the original words of the 1603 edition, which agree with an autograph copy of Baïf's poems, except in modifying his experimental orthography. The original has barlines after each line of the poem. The metre fits into six-beat bars, divided into both 2 × 3 and 3 × 2. It appears to flow from one section to another without breaks. The original, however, has a minim rest in all parts at the beginning of each section, though not at the opening; there are also minim rests elsewhere, represented in this edition by commas.

36. Marenzio: *Crudel perche mi fuggi*

It could be argued that the unaccompanied Italian madrigal reached its peak in Marenzio. He was extremely prolific in the form, publishing over twenty books of them. He seems, in a way matched only by Monteverdi (whose shadow has concealed him), to be able to express the essence of every verbal phrase. He worked in various parts of Italy, settling in Rome for most of the 1590s, apart from obeying papal instructions to go to Warsaw in 1596. He was particularly influential in England, being the predominant composer represented in three anthologies published with English versions of the Italian texts: *Musica Transalpina* in 1588 and 1597 and Thomas Watson's *Italian Madrigals Englished* in 1590. In fact, twenty-three of the twenty-eight madrigals in Watson's collection are by Marenzio. Watson's contemporary fame as a poet did not last, but his skilful paraphrases of Italian were partly responsible for the tone of English madrigal verse in its heyday over the following twenty years. This text was set again by Wilbye in his first book (1598).
Source: Il quarto libro de madrigali a sei voci (Venice, 1587); *The first sett of Italian Madrigalls Englished, not to the sense of the originall dittie, but after the affection of the noate. By Thomas Watson* (London, 1590). When the Italian text was published by Guarini in his *Rime* in 1598, it began 'Lasso perche mi fuggi'. Performers of the English version will need to decide whether to underplay rhythmic features that relate to the Italian text but not the English; at bar 17, for instance, the second note needs to be unaccented with a crescendo to the fourth

beat, with 'death can as-' sung as a three-beat phrase across the barline. In bars 28–9 and 31–2, an *esclamazione* can be sung (see p. vii).

37. Marenzio: *Scaldava il sol*

The words of this madrigal are taken from a poem *Favola di Narciso* depicting a sultry summer's day with the god Pan lying asleep. The overall mood is magically caught and should not be broken by making the illustrations of detail too vivid. When there are quavers, there is always at least one part maintaining the slower pulse. In bar 53, the solitary 'sol' is an obvious piece of word painting; less obvious in this transposed edition is that it also set to a G, 'sol' in Italian.
Source: Luca Marenzio, *Il terzo libro de madrigali a cinque voci* (Venice, 1582).

38. Monteverdi: *O Mirtillo, Mirtillo, anima mia*

Monteverdi's madrigals first established his reputation, though now we hear his operas and church music far more frequently. He had an even greater flair than Marenzio for finding musical ideas that embody both the sound and the sense of each phrase of text. Monteverdi worked from 1590 to 1612 at the court of Mantua, then spent the rest of his life in charge of music at the Basilica of San Marco in Venice. Most of his madrigals were written during his Mantuan period, and by 1603 he was absorbing (or initiating) the new style, which split the voices that were normal for madrigals into smaller groups, most often duets or trios. Here much of the texture is that of a duet, with a third voice supplying the harmony. A continuo part was added in a reprint published in Antwerp in 1615; this follows the lowest sounding part and differs little from the bottom line of the keyboard accompaniment printed here.

The words are from Act III of Guarini's famous play *Il pastor fido*. It is difficult now to imagine why this undramatic story of pastoral lovers had such fame in the 1590s and 1600s and beyond (Handel wrote an opera on it in 1712). Excerpts were used as the text for countless madrigals, perhaps because they were easily detachable and the generalized expressions of passion were not dependent on any specific knowledge of why Amarilli (whose words are set here) and Mirtillo are parted. Although the top two parts were notated in the same clef, they have distinctly terraced ranges, so have been allocated to soprano and alto. In choral performances, some low altos should join with the first tenors and some baritones with the second tenors. Transposition down a tone would help the tenors if the basses can manage an E♭ in bar 2.
Source: Monteverdi, *Il quinto libro de madrigali* (Venice, 1605). *Variants:* 4 iv 3: ♮ in original / 5ff: original 'vedesti' / 55 and 61: we have retained the capitalization of 'Amor' in the Italian text, though visualizing a Cupid is unlikely to help a modern singer.

39. Monteverdi: *Ohimè so tanto amate*

This was a notoriously revolutionary piece in its day, either breaking or stretching (depending on your viewpoint) the conventions of polyphonic writing. It was difficult to sing, too: how did a soprano manage bar 2 from a single voice part, not a score? Guarini's text is an independent poem.

Source: Monteverdi, *Il quarto libro de madrigali* (Venice, 1603). *Variants:* 4 i 1: the cautionary ♮ is in the original edition; without it, singers would have sung *eb''*, avoiding the tritone above the bass *Bb* / 49–end: original inconsistent in giving 'dolc'' or 'dolci' / 57 iv 1–2: ♩., no rest.

40. Monteverdi: *Lamento d'Arianna*

This is the first and among the greatest of dramatic laments. It is the only surviving portion of Monteverdi's opera *Arianna*, performed in 1608 as part of the celebrations in honour of the return of the heir to the Duke of Mantua, Francesco Gonzaga, with his new bride, Margaret of Savoy. Arianna had helped Theseus escape from the labyrinth at Cnossos, where her father, Minos, King of Crete, had imprisoned him; but he abandoned her on the island of Naxos on his way home to Athens. According to the official report of the events, 'In the lament which Ariadne sings on the rock when she has been abandoned by Theseus, which was acted with so much emotion and in so piteous a way that no one hearing it was left unmoved, there was not one lady who did not shed some little tear at her beautiful plaint'. The lament circulated widely, and Monteverdi published an edition with Latin words as a Lament of the Madonna (edition by King's Music). He also made this more complex version with the texture reworked for five voices, turning a masterpiece in the new, monodic style into the older form of the polyphonic madrigal.

Source: Monteverdi, *Il sesto libro de madrigali a cinque voci . . . con il Basso continuo per potersi Concertare nel Clavicembano & altri stromenti* (Venice, 1614, reprinted 1615 and 1620). The continuo partbook is called 'Basso continuo' on the title-page but 'Partitura' at the top of each page. All the original 'figures' (sharps for major chords, flats for minor) have been retained. The single-line part is supplemented here by what is predominantly a reduction of the voice parts. It can be used as a rehearsal accompaniment for piano or as the basis of a harpsichord part. Players using the early editions may have had only a figured bass part in front of them, but there is evidence that players copied out scores (as Schütz recommended to German organists) or followed the movement of the voice parts quite closely by ear. There is no need for a string instrument to play the continuo bass. The work can be performed unaccompanied, especially if sung chorally. Occasionally the tactful exchange of a few notes with the tenor may avoid altos having to sink too low.

For further information, see the introduction and critical commentary to the separate edition, Oxford Choral Classics, OCCO 24.

41. Morley: *My bonny lass she smileth*

If you wanted to film a scene of an Elizabethan family amusing themselves by singing a madrigal, you would probably have them sing either this or the following Morley ballett, two of the most recognizable examples of vocal ensemble music of the period. It was Thomas Morley who set the agenda for the brief but intense

flowering of English madrigals in the 1590s and 1600s, naturalising in particular the lighter forms prevalent in Italy at the time. His balletts led to an epidemic of 'fa la la'-ing, extending their use from the very lightest type of secular song to association with serious and even sombre texts. His *First Book of Balletts* of 1595 was popular enough to need a reprint in 1600 and it was also issued in 1595 with Italian words; a German version was prepared by Valentin Haussmann (Nuremberg, 1609). Several of the pieces are based extremely closely on *Balletti a cinque voci* by Giovanni Giacomo Gastoldi (1554–1622), published in 1591 (see no. 21). *Sing we and chant it* is very similar to the first *balletto* in that publication, though Morley is a little more subtle. *Now is the month of maying* has no such precise model, but has strong similarities to *So ben mi ch'a bon tempo* by the other leading Italian composer of vocal dances, Orazio Vecchi (1550–1605), from his *Selva di varie ricreatione* (1590). The Italian *balletti* were genuine dance music: a choreography for *So ben mi ch'a bon tempo* survives in Negri's *Le gratie d'Amore* (1602). They were also played as well as sung. The manner of instrumental participation in England is less certain, despite such phrases as 'apt for voices and viols' on title pages of some editions. The tendency towards elaboration and irregularity of phrase in the English balletts suggests that they were not danced.

Notating dynamic changes (whether in print or pencil) for the four times (six times for no. 42) that each section is sung would be confusing. The dynamic can change at each double bar, or the 'fa la la's can be sung at a different dynamic from the preceding texted section. The same pattern can be used for each verse, or they can be varied. It is fun (and good discipline) not to notate them but to respond to the conductor's indication without advance warning. If an audience is responding well, tease it by throwing in an extra repeat or an unexpected dynamic at the end. The ease of imposing dynamic levels should not impede the natural rise and fall within the phrases. 'Fa' should be stressed, especially if it is off the beat; unstressed syllables at the ends of phrases (e.g. 'smileth') should be taken very lightly, especially when sung *f*.

Source: Of Thomas Morley the first booke of balletts to five voyces (London, 1595). In both pieces, each verse is printed out in full without repeats but only the first verse is underlaid. *Note:* the triple-time section (bars 17–25) has the time signature **3** and black notation; note values are halved.

42. Morley: *Now is the month of maying*

May Day was celebrated widely; indeed, some customs persisted into the twentieth century, though their demise was probably hastened by the day's association with demonstrations by the urban proletariat. At dawn, maydew was gathered for medicinal and cosmetic purposes; later there were games and dancing round the maypole (a practice that needs some skill to prevent the ribbons getting tangled). Barley-break could be a complicated game, if played in the manner recounted in Sir Philip Sidney's *A Shepherd's Tale* (*Arcadia*, 1598); no doubt similar symbolic games were staged when

Queen Elizabeth went a-maying. But the word was also used for a simpler game of tag.

Source: Of Thomas Morley the first booke of balletts to five voyces (London, 1595). At the opening, we have omitted minim and crotchet rests. *Variants:* 4 ii 3: no ♮ in the source, but the notation of accidentals is precise, with a ♯ before every other *f'* in the phrase, so the absence of a ♯ is significant; similarly 10 ii 2 and 12 iii 2 (*c♮"*). See also note to no. 41 for performance suggestions.

43. Parry: *Music, when soft voices die*

Parry came from an affluent background. After reading law and history at Oxford, he became an underwriter at Lloyds, but in 1877 was sufficiently confident of his musical abilities to abandon his career. By the 1890s, he was a leading figure in many branches of music—musicologist, administrator, composer—and in 1898 he was knighted. He was highly regarded as a teacher by composers such as Vaughan Williams, but his compositions have fared less well. His anthem *I was glad* was sung at all twentieth-century British coronations; a tune from his oratorio *Judith* become popular as a hymn tune ('Dear Lord and Father of mankind') and his setting of William Blake's *Jerusalem* has won favour as a patriotic song with the Women's Institute and the Promenade Concerts. His *Songs of Farewell*, although not church music, are more appropriate for a volume of sacred music.

Source: Six Modern Lyrics, set as Part-Songs . . . 6 (Novello, London, 1897). Novello's Part-Song Book (Second Series), PSB no. 766. *Variant:* 14 i and iv: ＜ in the original edition.

44. Passereau: *Il est bel et bon*

The few surviving biographical references to Passereau show him to have been a church singer, but apart from one motet, only chansons survive. For the modern singer, he is a one-work man, and this onomatopoeic piece is invariably popular. A modern performance style has evolved, treating it as a patter song with the refrain sung quietly, ending virtually inaudibly, and the other sections always beginning louder than they end. Singers who enjoy this chanson should try the two rather longer pieces by Passereau's contemporary Janequin, *Le chant des oiseaux* and *La bataille*.

Source: Vingt et huyt chansons musicalles (Paris, 1534) (*RISM 1534¹¹*).

45. Pearsall: *Lay a garland*

Pearsall was a lawyer who moved to Germany in 1825 for the sake of his health. He had become interested in discovering early music and composing in the Renaissance style. His imitations of Morley's madrigals were performed by the new Bristol Madrigal Society, which was set up in 1837 while he had returned to sort out the family estate at nearby Willsbridge. He is best known for his arrangement of *In dulci jubilo*. Madrigal singers find *Lay a garland* the most effective of the nineteenth-century partsongs, its relationship to earlier styles not being so self-conscious as in some of Pearsall's other music. It was written in 1840 to words taken from Beaumont and Fletcher's play *The Maid's Tragedy*, Act

II, scene 1, though changed from first to third person. Dating from around 1610, the play was performed fairly regularly until the Victorian period, so Pearsall could well have seen it. It is one of those gory tragedies in which everyone finishes up dead, though 'happily ever after' adaptations diminished the play's original gloom. The song is sung by Aspasia, whose betrothed has been forced to undertake a marriage of convenience to the king's mistress. The chief performance problem of Pearsall's setting is tempo. It is usually sung by small choirs used to the current style of singing early music, who probably take it faster than Pearsall would have done; listeners too are used to faster tempi for music of the Renaissance, and performing it too slowly may emphasize its origin in the 1830s and separate it from the style to which it relates.

Source: autograph manuscript, British Library, Add. MSS 38544, fols. 39–42: pencil draft overlaid by inked final version. Heading 'Lay a Garland on her hearse, an Eight-part Madrigal, written 4th June 1840 by R. L. Pearsall of Willsbridge'. A few pencil marks suggest that Pearsall thought of adding a Latin text, 'O salutaris', but instead copied it out afresh with the text 'Tu es Petrus' (Add. MSS. 38540). The posthumous edition published in the 1880s by Novello (Novello's Part-Song Book, Second Series, vol. 11, PSB no. 320.) has many dynamics added by its anonymous editor; we have included those in the piano reduction. The inconsistent slurring of the MS has been retained. *Variants:* iii and iv: alto clef; v and vi: tenor clef / 11 iv: ♩ in pencil sketch, but stem not inked over / 16 iv 3: ♭ (unbracketed) in MS / 20 ii: this is the only hairpin in the MS / 32 i and iv 2: D♭s in the pencil version but the flats are not inked over; the ♭ in 34 iv 2, however, is inked / 36–7 vi: separate slurs from *g'* to *f'* and from *f'* to *e'* / 41 vii: additional slur from *g* to *f*.

46. Pilkington: *Rest, sweet nymphs*

Nothing is known of Pilkington's early life, but when he took his Bachelor of Music degree at Oxford in 1595 he claimed he had been a student of music for sixteen years. From 1602 he worked at Chester Cathedral, as both musician and cleric. In addition to a book of airs, he published two books of madrigals, in a retrospective style suggesting that provincial musical circles were less subject to fashion than those in London. This is a rather more playful treatment of the sleep theme than Dowland's in the second verse of *Weep you no more, sad fountains* (no. 13).

Source: Francis Pilkington, *The First Booke of Songs or Ayres* (London, 1605). Verses 2 and 3 not underlaid in original. Lute part omitted. *Note:* 1–5: the stress should follow the verbal stress of each verse, irrespective of the barlines. The second crotchet of bar 1, for instance, needs some weight, the first note of bar 2 is unstressed for verses 2 and 3. *Variants:* 3, 9, 20: editorial accidentals correspond with lute tablature / 2 iii 1: ♮ / 6 i 1: 'Whilst'. ii, iii, iv: 'Whiles'; 2nd verse: 'Whiles' / 8 ii: 'pleasant' / 8 iii 2: *c'* in lute part / 13: time signature **3** / 13–14: the original barring is | Sleep sweetly, sleep sweetly | let nothing affright ye |. This distorts the stress of the text, so we have displaced each note a step earlier, beginning the triple time at the end of bar 12 and adding a rest at the end of bar 14 / 15: time signature **c**; if the rest feels redundant, it may be omitted, though it can help to maintain the calm mood and make it easier not to accent the minim.

47. Rore: *Ancor che col partire*

Rore was the most adventurous of the Italian madrigal composers in the years around the middle of the sixteenth century. He went from Flanders to Italy in the early 1540s, and became director of the important musical centre of the court of Ferrara in 1545. He returned to Flanders in the late 1550s, then spent his last few years at Parma. *Ancor che col partire* was one of those pieces which, presumably because everyone knew them, became examples in manuals of ornamentation (see also no. 48): singers who wish to sing more than the notes that are written (or those who wish to alternate instrumental settings to make a varied concert) should consult Girolamo Dalla Casa, Giovanni Bassano, and others, *Divisions on 'Ancor che col partire' for solo instrument or voice and continuo* (London Pro Musica Edition, 1986, LPM REP11). The music shows a contrapuntal flexibility that was new to the madrigal at the time. The poem is conventional enough, but the fact that it was believed to be by a nobleman who had recently died may have drawn attention to it. Like so many 'facts', however, recent scholarship has questioned the ascription: the words Rore set differ somewhat from the version explicitly ascribed to Alfonso d'Avalos in Cimello's *Libro primo de canti a quatro voci* (1548).

Source: first published in Perissone Cambio, *Primo libro di madrigali a quattro voci . . . con alcuni di Cipriano Rore* (Venice, 1547); also in Rore's *Il primo libro de madrigali a quatro voci* (Ferrara, 1550, and many reprints). Note values have been halved, so do not be tempted to begin too quickly; use bars 30 onwards to find a suitable tempo.

48. Sandrin: *Douce mémoire*

Sandrin was probably an actor named Pierre Regnault who acquired the name Sandrin from a play in which a character of that name, a cobbler, replied to every question by singing the opening of a chanson. He worked as a church musician, but all his surviving music is secular. This is one of fifty chansons by him published between 1538 and 1549. It became extremely popular, and like Rore's *Ancor che col partire* (no. 47), it was used as a model to illustrate how to ornament. The Spaniard Diego Ortiz used it in his *Tratado de glosas* (1553), printing it in something like its original version (there are some differences from the 1538 edition) and with several embellished settings for viol. Twenty-four versions have been brought together in George Houle, *Doulce memoire: a study in performance practice* (Indiana University Press, 1990). Lassus and Rore wrote masses based on the chanson. François I was king of France from 1515 and, like his contemporary Henry VIII (whom he met at the Field of the Cloth of Gold), he had a strong interest in the arts. He devoted some of his enforced leisure during his imprisonment after the Battle of Pavia (1525) to writing chanson texts.

Source: Second livre contenant XXVII chansons nouvelles (Paris, 1538), and *Le Parangon des chansons. Second livre contenant XXXI chansons nouvelle[s]* (Lyons, 1538). *Variants:* the edition is based on the latter, but with editorial accidentals based on Ortiz's more explicit notation. But it is not clear whether Ortiz is merely modernizing the notation or updating the style, and some may prefer to ignore his sharp in bars 3 and 16. Later sources have major chords in bars 13 and 26 / 6 and 19 ii 2–3: ♩ / 29 iv 1: *d*.

49. Schubert: *Der Tanz*

This was written to tease Irene von Kiesewetter, the daughter of Raphael Georg Kiesewetter, a leading Austrian administrator and pioneering musicologist, for her passion for dancing. Irene was a proficient pianist, who sometimes played with Schubert. Various dates have been allocated to this short work: early in 1828 is currently favoured, just after a short Italian cantata dated 26 December 1827 which Schubert wrote to celebrate her recovery from an illness (D 936; this work is D 826). The poem is ascribed to 'Schnitzer', who may be Kolumban Schnitzer von Meerau.

Sources: autograph manuscript, Vienna Stadtbibliothek, MH 37/c. This has no heading and has only verse 1 underlaid, with a note that verse 2 is to be sung to the same melody. Verse 2 is in a contemporary MS in the Archiv der Gesellschaft der Musikfreunde in Vienna (Witteczek-Spaun Collection, vol. 31, pp. 115–22) which contains a score (headed 'der Tanz von Schnitzer') with verse 1 underlaid and a set of vocal parts with the text of both verses. *Notes:* original vocal clefs, C1, C3, C4, F4. We have placed the dynamics in the piano part in the same place as in the vocal parts, although the MS places them after the barline at 16/17, 20/21, and 24/25. Perhaps the piano introduction should be played again at the end.

50. Senfl: *Ach Elslein, liebes Elselein*

Senfl was the leading composer of German song in the early years of the sixteenth century. The repertoire is generally called the *Tenorlied*, since the melody was usually in the tenor. In this example, however, the traditional melody is given to the soprano. Senfl was a choirboy at the court of the Emperor Maximilian from 1496, staying there after his voice changed. He probably studied with Isaac (see no. 28) and succeeded him in 1513. After Maximilian's death in 1519, the new emperor, Charles V, was more interested in his own Spanish musicians, and he secured a position worthy of his status only in 1523, when he joined the chapel of Wilhelm IV of Bavaria at Munich. During his life he was chiefly famous for his Latin music, but German scholars reviving his music in the last century paid greater attention to his secular songs. This is his simplest and most popular.

Source: Der erst Teil. Hundert und ainundzweintig newe Lieder (Nuremberg, 1534) (*RISM* 1534[17], collated with 1536[8] and other sources in accordance with the version printed in *Das Erbe deutscher Musik*, vol. 15 [= *Senfl Werke*, vol. 4]).

51. de Sermisy: *Au joli bois*

Claudin de Sermisy spent most of his life working for the French royal chapel. His extensive body of church music has mostly been ignored by scholars and performers, but he is acknowledged as a leading composer of a style which emerged in Paris in the late 1520s and was published extensively there by the printer Attaingnant. Indeed, of the thirty-one pieces in Attaingnant's first anthology of chansons, over half are by Claudin. The Parisian chanson is, in its archetypal form, loosely homophonic and appears to set only one verse of a poem, although longer versions circulated in independent poetic anthologies. This poem was published in an undated pamphlet entitled *S'ensuyvent viii. belles chansons nouvelles* (reprinted in Brian Jeffery, *Chanson verse of the early renaissance*, vol. 1, pp. 198–204) with three verses. The main difference in the first verse is the opening ('Au bois de dueil') and bars 19–20 ('Dans un vert pré'). Brian Jeffery points out the similarity of the style to that of Clément Marot. The poem, with its distinctive metre, exists in various parodies, including a versification of the ten commandments (see Dorothy Packer, 'Au boys de dueil and the Grief-Decalogue', *Journal of Musicology*, 3, 1984, pp. 19–54.) There is a six-voice reworking by Gombert.
Source: Trente et une chansons musicales (Paris, 1529) (*RISM* 1529²). The transposition theoretically requires a signature of two sharps, except that it looks wrong. A small natural before a note indicates where the editor believes the note would have been flattened.

52. Stanford: *The blue bird*

Stanford was the conductor of The Bach Choir in London from 1885 to 1902. The choir had been formed in 1875 to give the first English performance of Bach's Mass in B minor. Its instigator was a lawyer and amateur singer, a great-nephew of the author of *Kubla Khan* and *The Ancient Mariner*, Arthur Duke Coleridge (Duke is a name, not a title). His daughter Mary was extremely well educated (see note to 53) and had considerable gifts as a poet; after her death her friend Sir Henry Newbolt published 237 of her poems. *L'oiseau bleu* is assigned to 1894 by Theresa Whistler, the editor of *The Collected Poems of Mary Coleridge* (London, 1954).
Source: The blue bird (Stainer and Bell, London, 1910). The original accompaniment, slightly modified here, is headed 'Pianoforte. For practice only'. The practice of having the soprano part sung by a soloist, with the other sopranos singing the upper alto part, is effective but not indicated by the composer. Original time signature: **c**.

53. Stanford: *Heraclitus*

Stanford was the son of a Dublin lawyer. He studied in Cambridge, Leipzig, and Berlin and was professor of composition at the Royal College of Music in London from its opening in 1883; he was also professor of music at Cambridge from 1887. William Johnson was from 1845 to 1872 a fellow of King's College, Cambridge, and a fine teacher of classics at Eton (where he wrote the *Eton Boating Song*). His career came to an abrupt end when the headmaster discovered a letter to a pupil written in rather too affectionate a manner. He changed his name to Cory, married in 1878, and settled in Hampstead in 1882, where he taught classical Greek to a group of young women, including Mary Coleridge (see note to no. 52). Stanford headed his setting of *Heraclitus* 'Poem by William Cory', but Cory's poem is in fact a literal translation of a poem from the Greek Anthology, a collection of lyric poems, some dating back as far as the seventh century BC, assembled in the tenth century AD, amplified in the fourteenth, and discovered by Western scholars in the seventeenth. Book 6 no. 80 is ascribed to Callimachus, a poet who worked in Cyrene and Alexandria in the third century BC and may have lived from *c*.320 to *c*.240 BC. It is an imaginary epitaph for a contemporary poet, Heraclitus (not to be confused with the philosopher Heraclitus of Ephesus, who lived about 250 years earlier), who died in or before 266 BC.
Source: Heraclitus (Stainer and Bell, London, 1908). The original accompaniment, slightly modified here, is headed 'Pianoforte. For practice only'. Original time signature: **c**.

54. Sullivan: *The long day closes*

Sullivan had achieved some success as a musician before the first of his successful operettas with W. S. Gilbert, *Trial by Jury*, in 1876. He studied at Leipzig, and his graduation exercise, music for *The Tempest*, immediately brought him fame, if not fortune. As Elgar was to do later, he won commissions from the provincial oratorio circuit, and he was appointed principal of the National Training School for Music. *The long day closes* dates from 1868 and was one of a group of seven songs for male voices. The words are by Henry Chorley, one of the leading musical journalists of the day, who had favoured the young Sullivan. The version for mixed voices appeared after his death, in 1902. It is such a typical image of Victorian words and music that we could not omit it, even if this is not as Sullivan composed it.
Source: The long day closes; four-part song . . . arranged for S. A. T. B. (Novello, London, 1902), Novello's Part-Song Book (Second Series), PSB no. 894.

55. Vaughan Williams: *Three Shakespeare Songs*

Vaughan Williams probably reached the peak of his fame with his Sixth Symphony, first performed in 1948. It seemed to have a powerful extra-musical message about the violence and bleakness of the post-war world. However, the composer himself referred to Prospero's farewell speech at the end of *The Tempest*, and there are several reminders of the music of the symphony in this choral work, written for a competitive festival in June 1951 of the British Federation of Music Festivals.
Source: Three Shakespeare Songs for S.A.T.B. unaccompanied (Oxford University Press, 1951). A few minor changes have been made to the piano reduction to bring it into closer conformity with the voice parts, though no attempt has been made to follow the details of the dynamics. The slurs in the piano part of song 1, 21–4 reveal a characteristic three-quaver pattern such as Vaughan Williams uses at the opening of the Sixth Symphony. *Variant:* Song 2, 25 i: second soprano note omitted from the first edition.

56. Vautor: *Sweet Suffolk owl*

Vautor worked for the Villiers family, and his single publication is dedicated to George Villiers, Duke of Buckingham, James I's notorious favourite. The family seat was at Brooksby in Leicestershire, moving to Goadby in the same county when George Villiers senior died in 1606. If he was still connected with the family after Buckingham's rise, he would probably have been based in London. He became an Oxford Bachelor of Music in 1616. His music shows a degree of independence from the standard madrigal style, as this example shows. 'Dight' (bar 16) means 'dressed'. The certainty once thought to exist in proportional notation has been under question of late so there is discretion in the relationship between duple and the triple note values at bars 51–63. The time signature is ₵ over 3₁. The options are bar = bar, half bar = bar, or crotchet = minim. On the grounds that the 'souls' in 61–3 should be the same length as in bar 64, I favour the second. Various English pieces (especially by Jenkins, who was based in East Anglia) suggest the sounding of bells in a similar manner to this passage.
Source: The First Set: being Songs of divers Ayres and Natures . . . Apt for Vyols and Voyces (London, 1619). *Variant:* 57 iv 1: ○· (no rest).

57. Weelkes: *a. Thule, the period of cosmography*
b. The Andalusian merchant

Weelkes published four sets of madrigal books between 1597 and 1608, including some of the most ambitious pieces in the repertoire. Unlike other leading composers of his time, he kept clear of London, working at Winchester College from 1598 then moving to Chichester Cathedral in 1602, the year in which he was awarded an Oxford Bachelor of Music degree. His life went into a decline; whether alcoholism was the cause or consequence is not known. *Thule, the period of cosmography* is rare for an English madrigal in being in two sections; they are linked by common conclusions, announced by the chord change on 'wondrous'. The text calls on the discoveries of the explorers, and needs some explanation for the modern singer and audience. Iceland (Thule), at the end of the world, boasts a volcano (Mount Hecla) as powerful as three-cornered Sicily's Mount Etna. Cochineal is a scarlet dye made from the dried body of the female *coccus cacti*, a scale insect that lives on the *opuntia Coccinellifera* cactus native to Mexico. 'China dishes' at this period means crockery actually from China. Fogo probably refers to Fogo Island, a volcanic island in the Atlantic (one of the Cape Verde islands); the identification with Terra del Fuego, the southern tip of South America, is unlikely.
Source: Madrigals of 5. and 6. parts, apt for the Viols and voices (London, 1600). *Variant:* the second part, 6 iii 5: 're-' a note earlier.

58. Wilbye: *Draw on, sweet Night*

Wilbye spent much of his life working for the Kytson family, partly at Hengrave Hall in Suffolk, but also at their house in London, so he was able to keep in touch with musical developments at court. This anonymous poem presents fine phrases for musical setting though is somewhat clumsy as verse. The third line, 'My life so ill through want of comfort fares', means 'My life fares so ill because of lack of comfort'. The rhyme 'melancholy'/'wholly' is weak, even if '-choly' is pronounced like 'wholly'; Wilbye covers this awkwardness by making the listener feel that the return of 'Sweet Night, draw on' is the conclusion of the first verse rather than the beginning of the second. Singers need to be careful not to land heavily on the final syllable of feminine rhymes, popular in madrigal verse in imitation of Italian. The tempo can easily sag: two beats in a bar should be maintained throughout, otherwise it is difficult to sing 'and while thou all in silence dost enfold' and 'I then shall have best time for my complaining' as single phrases.
Source: The Second Set Of Madrigals To 3. 4. 5. and 6. parts, apt both for Voyals and Voyces (London, 1609). *Variants:* 59 iii 1: ♯ (= ♮) in original, since singers from a single partbook might expect such a leap to be a minor sixth / 63 vi 2: it is tempting to sharpen the c to match S1 in 61, but the original edition is quite accurate with regard to accidentals and there is nothing except a keen ear to suggest to the singer that it should be sharpened / 73–4 v: 'told' three notes earlier / 99 v 2: underlay 'when' for 'while' / 106–8 v: underlay from last note of 103 indicated by 'ij' (see Preface); by normal practice 'en-' should be placed under the second note of bar 106, but delaying the syllable to bar 108 articulates the leap of a fourth / 107 i 4: could perhaps be sharpened / 126 iii 4–end: underlay marked 'ij', so if text of previous phrase is repeated exactly, it should be 'for my complain - - - ing'.

59. Wilbye: *Weep, weep, mine eyes*

English music for weeping usually has Dowland's *Lachrimæ* theme somewhere: here it opens the tenor part. A curiosity is that only the bass sings the lady's name. This piece can easily drag: markers for a good tempo are to think of a forceful speed for bars 38–42 and to make it possible for the bass from bars 71 to the end to sound like a single phrase. A version for solo voice and continuo survives in a contemporary manuscript; an edition is published by King's Music.
Source: The Second Set Of Madrigals To 3. 4. 5. and 6. parts, apt both for Voyals and Voyces (London, 1609). The index uses the title *Weep, O mine eyes*, but in modern usage the 'O', which appears only in the tenor part, is omitted to avoid confusion with the four-voice madrigal that begins thus. *Variants:* 17–19 i: 'Weep heart, weep eyes', but other parts reverse the order of nouns for this, the third line of the poem / 32–7, alto underlay: 'ij' under last note of 33, 'a thou-sand' under first three notes of 34, then nothing until 38; perhaps repeat 'I die' on notes 2 and 3 of 33 / 64ff: 'Elysian' spelt 'Elizian' throughout / 64 and 66, ii, iii, v: the inconsistent lengths of 'plain' are thus in the original, but the parts should end the phrase together, a reminder not to take the notated lengths too literally.